"Thought that consulting was something you'd fill the spa[...] again! Elaine's latest book, *The New Consultant's Quick Star[...]* tools and guidance you need to become a successful independent consultant for the long haul!"

> Ken Blanchard, co-author of *The New One Minute Manager®* and *Leading at a Higher Level*

"Arguably the foremost authority on training consulting, Elaine Biech continues to build her impeccable reputation as a savvy, practical, no-nonsense consultant with this important update to her classic. She has produced a personal planning guide that will illuminate the path to consulting success and help you jumpstart your consulting business with practical ideas."

> Dr. Jim Kirkpatrick, co-author of Kirkpatrick's *Four Levels of Training Evaluation*

"I loved working with Elaine Biech, a consultant on some of our contracts. She struck fear in the hearts of major consulting contractors like Booz-Allen and Accenture. She is that good, and her costs are lower. I've seen her get a room full of leaders transformed from bitter enemies to friendly partners. If you are thinking about starting a consulting business, she began from the ground up and continues to flourish. I highly recommend her books and courses."

> David L. Winters, former division director, Office of Naval Research, author of *Taking God to Work*

"Elaine Biech has written a relevant book for getting started in the consulting business. The timing is right as we move into a world where organizations and people need more input and advice from the outside."

> Ingar Skaug, board chairman, Center for Creative Leadership and former VP, SAS

"Practical. Inspiring. Ethical. Wise. Essential reading for anyone starting a consulting practice. I wish I'd had this when I started out. This needs to be on every new consultant's desk."

> Jonathan Halls, author, *Confessions of a Corporate Trainer: An Insider Tells All*

"The best 'Cliff Notes' available for those new to consulting and an excellent refresher reference for the experienced."

> Pamela J. Schmidt, executive director, ISA

"Elaine Biech is right on the mark with her latest release. With bookshelves full of numerous 'how-to' titles, it is refreshing to find one that really is loaded with practical, easy-to-use information based upon Elaine's admirable consulting experience. If you are thinking of entering the consulting field and are looking for one easy-to-use manual, pick up a copy of *The New Consultant's Quick Start Guide*."

Joseph Ruppert, Captain, USN, retired

"A must-read for people who are considering a career in consulting. The book is filled with realistic and practical ideas—a great way to learn all the tricks of the trade from one of the best!"

Vicki L. Chvala, former executive vice president, American Family Insurance

"Anybody who wants to quit his or her day job to join the legions of free-agents and consultants needs this book. There are so many facets of the consulting business, and Elaine provides the quickest road to plan for success. This book will dramatically reduce your learning curve."

Kristin Arnold, president, Quality Process Consultants, Inc.

"A logical, step-by-step guide through the consulting jungle. Follow Elaine's lead as if your business life were depending on it!"

Linda Byars Swindling, "The Peacemaker" and co-author, *The Consultant's Legal Guide*

"Elaine Biech has done it again! For anyone considering leaving the corporate world to become a free agent, this practical book is enormously valuable. Even established consultants would do well to review and learn from Elaine's focused and efficient set of tools and principles. Save yourself a lot of time and effort—buy this book and use it before, during, and after you begin your consulting practice."

B. Kim Barnes, CEO, Barnes & Conti Associates, Inc.

"A quick start is no longer a luxury—it's a survival strategy! Elaine Biech's newest comprehensive resource can save you precious time and money when you need it the most. Learn from a 'master' who has built a very successful consulting business—you won't regret it!"

Ann Herrmann-Nehdi, author, *The Whole Brain Business Book*, board chair and Chief Thought Leader, Herrmann International

The New Consultant's

Quick
Start

Guide

The New Consultant's

Quick
Start

Guide

An Action Plan
for Your First Year
in Business

elaine biech

WILEY

Published by John Wiley & Sons, Inc., Hoboken, New Jersey.

Published simultaneously in Canada.

For general information on our other products and services or for technical support, please contact our Customer Care Department within the United States at (800) 762–2974, outside the United States at (317) 572–3993 or fax (317) 572–4002.

Wiley publishes in a variety of print and electronic formats and by print-on-demand. Some material included with standard print versions of this book may not be included in e-books or in print-on-demand. If this book refers to media such as a CD or DVD that is not included in the version you purchased, you may download this material at http://booksupport.wiley.com. For more information about Wiley products, visit www.wiley.com.

Library of Congress Cataloging-in-Publication Data:
ISBN 9781119556930 (Paperback)
ISBN 9781119556954 (ePDF)
ISBN 9781119556916 (ePub)

Cover image: © Studio-Pro/Getty Images
Cover design: Wiley

Printed in the United States of America

V10008931_032119

For Shane and Thad

You ensured that I learned

the value of a Quick Start

Contents

Acknowledgments

This book was "authored" by many wise and wonderful people. Thank you to everyone.

- Consultants who led the way and taught me all that I know: Geoff Bellman, Ken and Margie Blanchard, Peter Block, Elliott Masie, Ann Herrmann-Nehdi, Bev Kaye, Jim Kouzes, Peter Senge, and Jack Zenger.

- Matt Holt, editor and friend, for sending subliminal messages and then making a phone call to confirm the deal.

- Vicki Adang, Zach Schisgal, and Shannon Vargo, the team that answered all my crazy questions and made time for me. You make me look great.

- Dawn Kilgore, the best production editor in the business, for caring about her work and her authors.

- Rebecca Taff, for unraveling my entangled sentences, cutting contrary commas, and reducing redundancy.

- Dottie Dehart, publicist extraordinaire, and her team, who ensure that this book gets a quick start.

- Dan Greene, for keeping the world at bay while I wrote.

- Mentors and friends who believe in what I do: Kristin Arnold, Halelly Azulay, Dianna Booher, Justin Brusino, Steve Cohen, Kris Downing, Admiral

Godwin, Linda Growney, Jonathan Halls, Shirley Krsinich, Jenn Labin, Robin Lucas, Toni Lucia, Jennifer Martineau, Cat Russo, Pam Schmidt, Judye Talbot, and Kathy Talton.

- Clients, for allowing me to practice the business of consulting with you.

Elaine Biech
ebb associates inc
Norfolk, Virginia
April 2019

Introduction

Why This Guide?

Books make a difference in people's lives. Just last week I met Marin Burton, a senior faculty member at the Center for Creative Leadership, where I am on the board of governors. She shared that she first learned of me when she was a freshman at the University of Wisconsin. Marin had discovered the excitement of facilitation and developing others, much to the chagrin of her father, who wasn't certain she could make a living using these frivolous skills. Coincidentally, her father and I had a mutual friend who worked at S.C. Johnson in Racine. He recommended one of my books, *The Business of Consulting,* and Marin's father gave it to her. The book reassured both father and daughter that one could make a living in the field of consulting. Marin now has a PhD, develops global leaders, and still has the book and the note I wrote to accompany it 20 years ago.

There is more to this brief coincidence than that we both grew up in Wisconsin and that we are in the same profession that we both love. It is really about consulting. Consulting is not just about making a living. It is about making a difference. As a consultant you will have many Marin-Magic Moments. People will stop you at conferences and tell you how you changed their lives. After a project with a client, employees will tell you what a difference your support made in their departments. And you will bump into people after an event or a training class when they reiterate a simple statement that you said dozens of years before that sparked a vision for them.

Consulting is about making a difference in people's lives. It's about achieving your vision while helping others achieve their visions, too. This book gives you a quick start toward your vision. The book that Marin read ends with the words "Wish on paper, and it becomes a plan." This book, *The New Consultant's Quick Start Guide,* provides the paper that you may use for wishing.

This book can become your plan—your blueprint for a consulting start-up. It includes questions to stimulate your planning, worksheets to develop your plan, and ideas to keep you motivated and moving forward.

This book is a companion to *The New Business of Consulting*; however, you do not need to have a copy of that book to have success with this one. I do cross-reference the two books so that they make sense if you are using both.

We are providing a bonus for you related to *The New Business of Consulting.* You will find many of its checklists, assessments, templates, financial forms, and other tools in this book.

Why Consulting?

The gig economy has brought a renewed and swelling interest in consulting. It's an ideal time to consider the profession. Management consulting exceeds $250 billion, with over 700,000 consulting firms providing services across all facets of business globally. The industry grows every year. The introduction of the current gig economy and the rapid changes in demographics and advances in technology have led companies and talent to engage in profoundly new ways—and consulting is one of the keys to success.

More respected than ever. Freelance consulting is viewed as a win for companies and consultants alike. Businesses count on consultants to build an agile workforce. Consultants can provide the expertise on demand and are reimbursed for the amount of time they are required to be on the job. Even large consulting firms are getting in on the gig economy, recognizing that they cannot support the large cadre of consultants they've had on staff in the past. In fact, in 2016 PricewaterhouseCoopers (PwC) launched its Talent Exchange, an online platform that finds independent consultants with relevant skill sets to work on PwC projects.

Increased desire for job satisfaction. Working 9 to 5 has become less desirable, especially for the Millennial generation (and the baby boomers, too) who are looking for work that gives purpose and meaning to life while also offering a good salary, flexibility, and autonomy. This brings problems with it. Consultants usually know their content, but they rarely know how to run a business. This book closes that gap by offering tools and techniques to help an entrepreneur to also manage a successful consulting business.

Access to comparable and better salaries. Consulting in the gig economy gives you a chance to make more or the same amount of money that you would in a traditional role. I have helped hundreds of people start their consulting businesses, and their biggest downfall is not knowing how to charge for their expertise. With the right advice, consultants can create a profitable six-figure income and more. This guide can get any new consultant started down the right path.

Who Will Find This Guide Useful?

You will find this guide useful if you are thinking about trying your hand at becoming a consultant. Whether you intend to join the gig economy as a full-time freelance consultant or as a part-time side hustler, this guide walks you through the many issues you'll encounter in determining whether this profession is right for you. You will explore whether you have the required skills and attributes to be a successful consultant. You will rate yourself against other entrepreneurs. You will identify personal, professional, and financial considerations necessary to ensure a quick start. And you will also explore your preferred future to determine whether consulting will allow you to achieve your professional and personal life goals.

You may also find this guide useful if you are new to the consulting profession and want to upgrade your consulting business acumen. Perhaps you started your practice but didn't have time to develop a marketing plan. This guide presents questions for you to answer to create your marketing plan, and an overview of the ABCs of marketing puts the task in perspective. Perhaps you didn't take the time to write a business plan, and now you find yourself heading in many directions at the same time and wondering whether there's a better way. The guide walks you through the steps of developing a business plan. Perhaps you thought consulting would lead to more control of your life, but instead you find yourself drowning in paperwork and trying to balance a completely out-of-control schedule. The guide shares tips, tactics, and tools to bring both your paperwork and your schedule back under your control.

You will find this guide useful whether you have previously read *The New Business of Consulting* or not. If you have, you will be prepared for many of the activities, assignments, and exercises in this book. And you will have read the practical advice and the real-world examples that support the exercises. If you have not read *The New Business of Consulting,* this guide provides a painless, fill-in-the-blank, practical approach to setting up your consulting business. It takes you through the highlights of establishing your consulting business. Nevertheless, you may still wish to purchase *The New Business of Consulting* if you want a more comprehensive discussion of the topic.

How to Use This Guide

Are you wondering:

- What the heck will I consult about?
- How do I figure out how much to charge?
- Who will be my clients and how will I approach them?
- How do I get my name out there?
- What legal responsibilities do I have?
- Am I really ready for this?

If these are your questions, you are in the right place. This book will guide you through the start-up quagmire, which really isn't that complex at all—as long as you progress in a logical, systematic direction. And that's where I can assist. I have helped more than 500 consultants at various stages of their careers—and this isn't even how I make a living. I can help you, too.

I encourage you to write directly in this book. Ample room has been provided for you to write most of your permanent plans directly on the pages.

This book has been designed for you to begin with Chapter One and work in order through the chapters to the end. Naturally you have your own unique needs, so you may wish to pick and choose the chapters (as well as the activities) that seem most pertinent to your situation. Of course, you will be the best prepared and most assured of success if you work through the entire guide.

If you are contemplating the consulting profession, I encourage you to begin with the activities in Chapters One and Two. They focus on planning your consulting future and will help you determine whether consulting is truly for you. You may also wish to work through those two chapters if you are already a consultant and not enjoying it as much as you anticipated. You may be able to figure out why and what you can do to change.

Chapters Three and Four are critical to ensure that you spend enough time planning for your successful consulting practice. These chapters address business structure and revenue issues. Insurance has become more important than ever, so Chapter Four has a list of questions to guide discussions with potential insurance brokers. You'll also find an electronic resource to help you unravel the insurance mystery.

Chapter Five will walk you through developing your business plan. If you are already consulting and have skipped this step, it's never too late to go back and plan now. In fact, a lack of a business plan may be one of the reasons you are not enjoying consulting or perhaps not as successful as you desire. This guide uses a question format that makes putting your thoughts and ideas on paper quick and easy.

Chapter Six is chock-full of ideas for making the transition from an internal job to external consulting as painless as possible. You will appreciate a list of suggestions for creating a discussion with your boss about your future plans.

Chapter Seven is all about your office: the whats, wheres, hows, and whys of running an efficient office. Working out of your home may seem like the easiest choice you have to make, but is it? Working out of your home has some definite advantages; it also has some disadvantages. If you are consulting and have made a decision about location, you may still want to read this chapter to determine whether you've thought of everything. For example, this chapter offers ideas about planning for your technical requirements, such as electronic record keeping.

Chapters Eight and Nine focus on finding and acquiring clients. This information is worth reading at any stage of your business—unless you already have more work than you can handle. (And if that's the case, you may want to read Chapter Eight, "Growing Pains," in *The New Business of Consulting*.) Marketing is a lot of common sense with a touch of creativity. Often simply reading someone else's ideas will remind you of what you knew all along but aren't practicing. These chapters will remind you again. Review the section about your website. Many websites do not do what's necessary to grab potential clients' interest.

Chapter Ten is a lifesaver—both figuratively and literally. Surviving your first year of consulting is as much about the work you do as it is about the way you run the business and the way you take care of yourself. There's good advice here no matter how long you've been in business.

Chapter Eleven helps you focus on year two. Although you may not actually complete these exercises if you are just starting out, you may want to peek ahead to see how you will be expected to assess your progress. Suggestions for reviewing your first year with your family make this chapter well worth your time.

In addition to the chapter content, you will find a dozen places that indicate Quick Start Actions. These actions go beyond the content in the chapter—beyond the basics. You can think of these ideas as "extra credit," like you had in school. They are additional activities that will give you an even quicker start. Tips are scattered throughout the chapters that are hints to make something easier, or an URL where you can find additional information.

The material in this guide will no doubt stimulate other thoughts and ideas. You may capture those thoughts at the end of each chapter on the Quick Start Lists. Space is available for you to list the actions you'll take based on what you read, the ideas that were stimulated by the chapter, and the questions you need answered. These lists summarize the actions you'll need to take to move forward. A robust reading list and URLs that you can tap into to obtain additional information round out the book.

Welcome to the gig economy. Now let's get you off to a quick start so that you can experience why I say that consulting isn't about just making a living. It's also about making a difference.

First Things First: Why Consulting?

In this chapter you will

- Define consulting
- Identify the experiences, skills, knowledge, and attributes that will lead you to a successful consulting career
- Assess your consulting aptitude
- Identify your initial consulting focus
- Test your entrepreneurial attitude

Consulting: What Is It?

A consultant is a professional who provides unique assistance or advice to someone else, usually known as the *client*. The assistance is usually advisory, strategic, or tactical in nature. The work is defined by the consultant's expertise, the structure in which the consultant works, and the process the consultant uses.

Expertise is based on what a consultant knows and has experienced. It can be anything from gardening to the stock market; from astral projection to pig farming; from organization development to preventing child abuse; from manufacturing to mining emeralds.

The structure within which the consultant works varies. You can work for a firm—for example, one of the large worldwide accounting firms, all of which have consulting branches. You could also work for a small or medium-size consulting firm or with a partner in your own office. Other possibilities are working in a virtual organization with a loosely structured relationship with other consultants across states or even nations, working as a subcontractor to any of those I have listed, working by yourself from a home office, or any of a dozen other structures.

The process a consultant uses is usually within one of the steps of problem solving. For example, a consultant might help a client in these ways:

- *Identify the problem:* "Why aren't our online sales growing the way we anticipated?" A consultant might identify the problem as a wasteful use of resources or a lack of repeat business.

- *Identify the cause:* "What is causing limited repeat business?" A consultant might identify the cause as sales staff who are rewarded more for new than repeat business, as poorly designed electronic tracking systems, or as employees with poor customer service skills.

- *Identify the solution:* "How do we ensure that our employees have the skills they need?" A consultant might identify solutions such as hiring more highly skilled employees, offering higher compensation to attract and retain skilled employees, or using coaching to improve the customer service skills of current employees.

- *Implement the solution:* "How can we improve our employees' customer service skills?" A consultant might help implement a solution by designing and delivering customer service skills training, creating a mentoring program that encourages on-the-job skill sharing, or establishing a monitored customer call center that provides feedback to each employee.

Isn't it likely that an organization already has these skills within its workforce? Employees who can identify the problem, cause, and solution and then implement the solution? Yes, probably, but they still might hire you. In today's rapidly changing world, businesses count on consultants to build the agile workforce they need. Consultants can provide the expertise on demand and are reimbursed for what they've contributed.

As a consultant you will likely be more efficient, because you will bring related experience that you've gained on other projects. That shortens your learning curve. You will have the luxury of focusing solely on the assigned project or problem and will not need to spend time on the organization's internal meetings and tasks.

You might also bring a unique skill set or expertise to a client's problem. Consultants also offer a fresh objective point of view. With hundreds of other projects and valuable experience under your belt, you can provide an unbiased fresh approach.

To summarize, consultants' expertise, the structure in which they work, and the process they use define the work. Consultants' experiences usually lead them naturally to each of these three elements. Experience and education provide the expertise that leads them to the field in which they specialize. Experience in other organizations as well as the lifestyle a consultant chooses lead them to using the right consulting structure. And experience also provides the consultant with the process, usually based on what the consultant has used in past work or the process the consultant's company uses.

Why a Consulting Career?

Do you awake on Monday morning, hop out of bed, and say, "Job, I missed you over the weekend! I can't wait to get to work!"? You don't? Well then, perhaps you are holding the right book.

No one should have to get up in the morning and go to work. Instead, we should all be able to get up and go to play. That is, we should enjoy our work so much that it seems like play. Most of us, however, distinguish work (what we must do) from play (what we'd rather be doing). Unfortunately, most of us get up and go to work every morning and save what we'd rather be doing for later in the day or later in the week. Consulting affords the opportunity for your work to be what you'd rather be doing. How could that be? As a consultant you will have:

- The flexibility to determine when you work, where you work, with whom you work, and what kind of work you do

- The opportunity to use the skills, experience, knowledge, and expertise that you possess and enjoy using

- Control over how much money you will earn

- A chance to do more meaningful work, make a difference in the world, and address that greater calling that comes from within

- An opportunity to travel—beyond fighting the traffic on your daily trek to the office

- The challenge to do more complex, exciting, or difficult work, to learn and grow

- The opportunity to manage and stabilize your own career in the current chaotic workplace

- The ability to live in a different location

Life is too short to sit in traffic! Or to do anything less than what you really want to do. I grew up on a farm in Wisconsin with a strong entrepreneurial spirit. I knew that I would never be a good employee: organizations didn't move fast enough for me; they were risk averse, and did little to release my creative spirit. I knew that consulting was an opportunity for me to take risks, try my own ideas, and be 100 percent responsible for my successes and my failures. Unfortunately, even when people are given a chance to create the kind of work they wish to pursue, they are sometimes unable to do so because there are so many choices. This book will help you begin to narrow those choices by identifying your experiences (opportunities for learning), your competencies (skills and knowledge), and your aptitude (natural talents and personal qualities).

And of course, it isn't all good. The drawbacks include a lack of regular paycheck and benefits, a lack of support services, and working alone. A lack of IT support is a big one for me. I remember spending two days writing my first very large proposal on my Apple IIe and losing the entire thing in two minutes. Needless to say, I learned to print as I went along, adding to lots of other lessons all new consultants learn.

So are you still interested in a consulting career? In the next sections you will explore the experiences, competencies, and attributes that will help define your consulting role. Let's begin by identifying the experiences you have had that would lead you to pursue a consulting career.

Explore Your Experiences

To begin to narrow your consulting choices, examine the expertise you've gained over the years. Although it's sometimes difficult to name your own expertise, you can easily identify experiences you've had. The skills and knowledge you've gained from your experiences help define your consulting role. (We will further explore the structure you will consider in Chapter Four to round out your role definition.)

Identify all the industries in which you have worked:

Identify all the volunteer experiences you've had:

Identify the organizational levels with which you have experience:

Review your various breadth and depth of experiences:

Identify the experiences that were the most rewarding and enjoyable:

Identify the experiences that were the most negative and unpleasant and that you wish to avoid in the future:

The experiences you've had provide you with a level of expertise for which clients will pay. Later in this chapter, you will use the information you have recorded to begin to identify your consulting focus.

Inventory Your Competencies

Everyone is very skilled or very knowledgeable about at least one thing. My plumber, Owen, for example, is the most knowledgeable person I know about anything that goes wrong with my plumbing. He can diagnose problems over the telephone and is highly skilled at making a quick repair.

Identify the knowledge and information you have. For example, a computer salesperson knows about sales and probably has also learned time management skills; a nurse may have taken workshops and read several books to improve communication skills.

List the things you do better than most other people:

List the things for which colleagues, employers, friends, and family come to you for assistance:

Identify special classes, courses, or seminars you've taken:

List special certifications, licenses, credentials, or warrants you hold:

List the problem-solving processes in which you are competent—for example, team building, Lean Six Sigma, root cause analysis, brainstorming, force field analysis, flowcharting, or dialogue facilitating:

List things you know a lot about:

The skills and knowledge you already possess in your area of expertise will help you define your consulting role later in this chapter.

Skills and Knowledge Required of Consultants

Consultants frequently underestimate the range and depth of skills required to lead a successful business. Most new consultants require more skills than they think they do. From the following list, circle the skills and knowledge for which you require improvement. Now check the three or four that when improved will make the greatest difference as you begin your consulting role:

☐ Prospecting and marketing

☐ Diagnosing client needs

☐ Gathering data through interviews and surveys

☐ Improving processes

☐ Playing roles such as trusted advisor, change agent, or initiator

☐ Managing expectations

☐ Addressing resistance

☐ Managing and facilitating change

☐ Identifying mutual expectations

☐ Estimating and pricing projects

☐ Completing paperwork on time

☐ Analyzing business data

☐ Using technology for research and to deliver services

☐ Designing solutions

☐ Developing talent

☐ Solving problems

☐ Building relationships

☐ Communicating with others

☐ Writing proposals and reports

☐ Conducting training

☐ Facilitating meetings

☐ Coaching managers

☐ Implementing intervention models

☐ Understanding and improving processes

Identify how you might gain the skills and knowledge you need:

Continuing to gain skills and knowledge is an investment in you. Every time you add to your knowledge base or increase your skills, you become more valuable as a consultant.

Assess Your Consulting Aptitude

Malcolm Forbes, publisher of *Forbes* magazine, has been credited with saying, "Too many people overvalue what they are not and undervalue what they are." Consulting takes a certain aptitude—those natural talents and personal qualities we all have. It might be the ability to solve a problem methodically or the creative talent to see the problem as a solution. Don't underestimate your natural talents and abilities. And if you know your weaknesses, also know that you can overcome them.

Are You a Match for the Profession?

The following statements identify the aptitude, natural talents, and personal qualities it takes to be a consultant. Check all with which you agree:

- ☐ I am a hard worker.

- ☐ I am in good health.

- ☐ I am a risk taker.

- ☐ I have a thick skin; being attacked as a pest, "beltway bandit," or con man does not bother me.

- ☐ I am persistent and determined.

- ☐ I am a big-picture person.

- ☐ I pay attention to details.

- ☐ I am an excellent communicator—oral and written.

- ☐ I am open-minded.

- ☐ I can think critically.

- ☐ I am an independent self-starter.

- ☐ I can promote myself.

- ☐ I can balance logic and creativity, big picture and details.

☐ I know my limitations.

☐ I can say no easily.

☐ I am self-disciplined.

☐ I am confident.

☐ I am competitive.

☐ I am flexible.

☐ I am a goal setter.

☐ I complete tasks.

☐ I am reliable and trustworthy.

☐ I like to work with people.

☐ I have passion for what I do.

Although the number of statements you checked will not guarantee success as a consultant, the statements you did not check point to challenges you will face as a consultant.

Which natural talents and abilities need the most improvement and attention?

Whom could you ask for a candid appraisal of your responses?

How will you adapt or acquire talents and aptitudes that aren't natural for you?

Whom could you ask for assistance?

Pull It Together: Your Initial Consulting Focus

You have spent time examining your experiences, your competencies, and your natural aptitudes. Now translate that into what a client might buy:

What experiences do you possess for which a client would be willing to pay?

What skills and knowledge do you possess for which a client would be willing to pay?

What natural talents and personal qualities do you possess for which a client would be willing to pay?

To what aspects of the problem-solving process would you be likely to contribute: identify the problem, identify the cause, identify the solution, or implement the solution?

What can you offer that will benefit clients? Check the items on this list that fit you, and then add several of your own.

- ☐ Diagnostic skills
- ☐ Listening skills
- ☐ Analytical skills
- ☐ Writing skills
- ☐ Research skills
- ☐ Organizational skills
- ☐ Strategic planning skills
- ☐ Investigative skills
- ☐ Change management experience
- ☐ Leadership skills
- ☐ Objectivity

- ☐ Flexibility
- ☐ Creativity
- ☐ New ideas
- ☐ Fast turnaround
- ☐ Meeting deadlines
- ☐ My publications
- ☐ My completed research
- ☐ My contacts
- ☐ My patents
- ☐ Knowledge
- ☐ Network of other experts

Experience with _____

_____

_____

Expertise in _____

_____

_____

Now take a first cut at describing your consulting work by completing the statement below. Some examples follow.

I am a _____ consultant who helps
my clients to _____ .

This benefits them _____ .

Examples

"I am a process improvement consultant who helps my clients become more efficient. This benefits them by reducing redundancy, increasing quality, decreasing time spent, and reducing cost to the customer."

"I am a web design consultant who helps my clients define and design websites. This benefits them by creating a professional-looking website in one-tenth the time and at half the cost."

We'll refine your niche in later chapters.

Entrepreneur Attitude: Do You Have What It Takes?

In addition to the experience, competencies, and aptitudes that make up your expertise, you must realize that becoming a consultant means that you are joining the entrepreneurial ranks. The Entrepreneur Attitude Survey shown here will tell you whether you have what it takes to become an entrepreneur.

The Entrepreneur Attitude Survey

Instructions: Rate yourself on the following qualities. They represent the thinking of several authors about the requirements of a successful business owner. Spend ample time pondering these questions and answer honestly. Rate yourself on a scale from 1 to 4 as follows:

1 = strongly disagree   3 = agree
2 = disagree   4 = strongly agree

Circle your answers.

1.	I usually try to take charge when I'm with others.	1	2	3	4
2.	I can do anything I set my mind to.	1	2	3	4
3.	I have a high tolerance for difficult situations.	1	2	3	4
4.	I believe I can always influence results.	1	2	3	4
5.	I am complimented on my ability to quickly analyze complex situations.	1	2	3	4
6.	I prefer working with a difficult but highly competent person rather than a friendly, less competent one.	1	2	3	4
7.	I can fire employees who are not producing.	1	2	3	4
8.	I'm willing to leave a high-paying, secure job to start my own business.	1	2	3	4
9.	I push myself to complete tasks.	1	2	3	4
10.	I can work long hard hours when necessary.	1	2	3	4
11.	I need to be the best at whatever I do.	1	2	3	4
12.	I do not become frustrated easily.	1	2	3	4
13.	I thrive on challenges.	1	2	3	4
14.	I become bored easily with routine tasks.	1	2	3	4

15.	I dislike being told what to do.	1 2 3 4
16.	I have a higher energy level than most people.	1 2 3 4
17.	I have held numerous leadership positions.	1 2 3 4
18.	I have the skills and enjoy accomplishing a complex task by myself.	1 2 3 4
19.	I can change my course of action if something is not working.	1 2 3 4
20.	I am seen as a creative problem solver.	1 2 3 4
21.	I can balance the big picture and details of a business at the same time.	1 2 3 4
22.	I can predict how actions today will affect business tomorrow and in the future.	1 2 3 4

23. I need at least _____ hours of sleep to function effectively.

1 = 8 hours 2 = 7 hours
3 = 6 hours 4 = 5 or fewer hours

24. I have at least _____ years of experience in the business I will start.

1 = 1 year 2 = 2 years
3 = 4 years 4 = 5 years

25. Over the past three years I have missed a total of _____ days of work due to illness.

1 = over 15 days 2 = 11–15 days
3 = 6–10 days 4 = 0–5 days

Scoring: Total the numbers you circled.

90 to 100	Go for it!
82 to 89	Good chance of success
74 to 81	Pretty risky
73 and below	Better continue to collect a paycheck

Although this survey can give you a general picture of what it takes to be a successful entrepreneur, only you can decide whether the move is right for you:

What did you learn about yourself?

What concerns you the most about being an entrepreneur?

What obstacles might you need to overcome? How will you do that?

What strengths will you parlay to your benefit? How will you do that?

Quick · · · · · · · · · · · · ▶ TIP

If your score was not as high as you would have liked it to be, call your local university or technical college to learn whether it offers classes in entrepreneurship. Ask for the reading list and syllabus. If you decide you do not wish to take such a course, you may at least want to read some of the books from the reading list to bolster your knowledge about what to expect.

Quick Start ACTION

Questions to Ask a Consultant

Before you begin the next chapter, interview a consultant. Consider it your take-a-consultant-to-lunch assignment. Gain as much information as you can about what it's like to be a consultant. You will not be able to ask all the questions listed, so prioritize those that are most important to you. I'm sure you will think of many others.

- How long have you been a consultant?
- How did you start?
- Why did you decide to become a consultant?
- How would you describe your consulting practice?
- How have you structured your business and what are the advantages and drawbacks of that structure?
- What do you do for clients? What problems do you solve?
- What's a typical project like?
- What's the biggest lesson you've learned as a consultant?
- Could you tell me about a time when you faced a difficult decision and how you handled it? What did you learn from it?
- What's a typical day or week like for you?

- What are the work/life balance issues for a consultant, and how do you address them?

- What marketing activities do you conduct?

- What process do you use for pricing projects?

- What's the greatest challenge for you as a consultant? The most frustrating?

- What would you do differently if you could start your consulting practice over again?

- How can I best prepare myself to become a consultant?

- What would you miss the most if you quit consulting?

- What should I have asked about that I didn't?

• •

After your interview, think about what you learned about consulting. How has it reinforced or changed your thoughts about consulting? Are you still interested in a consulting career?

Now that you have defined consulting and identified the experience, skills, knowledge, and attributes that you have that will lead you to a successful consulting career, you are ready to plan that career. Use the Quick Start Lists on the next page to capture your thoughts before moving on to Chapter Two. You will find Quick Start Lists at the end of each chapter. As you read future chapters and identify items you wish to remember, turn to the back of that chapter and record the actions you want to take, the ideas you think of, and the questions for which you want answers.

Quick Start **LISTS**

Actions I Will Take

Ideas I Have

Questions I Need to Answer

2

Planning Your Consulting Future

In this chapter you will

- Explore your preferred future
- Determine whether consulting will lead you to your professional and personal life goals
- Identify personal, professional, and financial considerations to ensure a quick start
- Identify the changes you will need to make
- Create a personal expense plan

Your Preferred Future

Why do you wish to become a consultant? What is it about consulting that appeals to you? How will consulting lead you to your preferred future? The reason to become a consultant is because you want to, and the first step is to explore why. Why do you want to become a consultant? How do you believe consulting will lead you to your preferred future? You are about to make a big decision—becoming an entrepreneur. It is usually difficult to separate entrepreneurs from their businesses; therefore, a plan for your consulting business should begin with a plan for you and your life. We touched on this in Chapter One. Now let's continue by describing your preferred future.

Describe Your Ideal Day

I remember working through this exercise more than 30 years ago in a two-week career exploration workshop. My description went something like this: "I awaken naturally to the sound of the surf and smell of the early morning ocean breeze. I sip a cup of gourmet coffee on the deck for half an hour as I skim the morning paper. As inspiration overwhelms me, I move to my desk that overlooks the ocean to continue writing my latest novel. I am lost in the task and the time passes quickly until 2 p.m., when I stop for a walk along the beach. That evening I prepare for the client with whom I will work the next day."

At the time, I was living on a dairy farm in the middle of Wisconsin, with a small income from my fledgling consulting practice and no writing experience. I'm sure the people in the workshop with me were thinking, "Yeah, right! What a dreamer." Although I haven't written any novels yet, I do have over seven dozen published books to my credit, most written while gazing at the Atlantic Ocean or Chesapeake Bay, where I own property.

Describe Your Future

Take some time now to describe your preferred future:

Describe your ideal day. How does your day begin? How will you divide your time? How does your day end?

Describe your surroundings. Where do you live? What do you see when you look out your window? What kind of car do you drive?

Describe your perfect job. What are you doing? With whom? Where are you working? What do clients say about your work? What do colleagues say about you?

Describe the logistics more thoroughly. How much do you travel? Where? How often? Who travels with you? What is your office like? Where is it? What's the view outside your office window?

Describe the results of your work. What honors or awards have you received? What's your annual salary? What profit does your business make? How much is in your retirement account? Your savings account?

What do you do for pleasure daily, weekly, and annually? With whom? Where? For what length of time? What hobbies have you tried?

What vacations have you taken?

What do you do when you're alone? What are you reading? What are your day-dreams?

What are your top five personal (family, friend, relationship) goals?

1.

2.

3.

4.

5.

What are your top five professional goals?

1.

2.

3.

4.

5.

What are your top three health goals?

1.

2.

3.

What are your top three financial goals?

1.

2.

3.

Will Consulting Lead You to Your Life Goals?

To determine whether consulting will help you reach your goals, begin by ensuring that you know why you want to become a consultant.

Why Are You Considering Consulting?

You probably have many reasons for your choice. Examine the three categories listed here and determine what part each plays in your decision. Think in terms of percentage. Divide 100 percent among the three categories. For example, if you just lost your job and consulting is the only answer you can see, you might rank "necessity" as 100 percent. If you have always wanted to be your own boss and you see that you have skills that are in demand, you might rank "personality" as 70 percent and "opportunity" as 30 percent. Place a percentage in the blank in front of each category that relates to your reasons.

_____ *It's a necessity:* You need a way to make a living and you believe consulting offers that. Perhaps you prefer a 9-to-5 job but recognize that they aren't as stable as they once were; you can't find a match to your expertise in your locale; your experience is too specialized for available jobs; you're in a low-paying job and believe your expertise is worth more; you've been downsized out of a job; you've been laid off or fired; you see the writing on the wall and you need to take care of yourself; you've retired and want something to keep you busy; you'd like to try a side hustle to pick up some extra cash, perhaps part time; or other reasons that necessitate making money as a consultant. Generally the reason is a desire for a job or the money that a job brings.

_____ *You see an opportunity:* You see a situation that you can exploit. Perhaps your company uses consultants, and you know you could do what they do, make more money, and work fewer days than you do now; you spot a trend in your field that is creating great demand for someone with your experience and skills; you have a special expertise for which there is a shortage; you have contacts, patents, or published works that you think are more valuable in another venue; consulting seems like an inexpensive and easy start-up; you want to travel; you want to live in a different location and see consulting as a way to get you there; or you see other unique options that could turn into business opportunities. Generally you could continue to do the job you are doing now, but want to take the risk.

_____ *Your personality demands it:* You want to consult. You would rather have your own business, no matter what the consequences are. Perhaps you are disillusioned with your current employer and know you could do it better yourself; big business moves too slowly for you; you need a creative outlet; you want to make a difference in the world and are not concerned about making as much money as you now make; you want to be independent; you want freedom from the daily grind; you want to be your own boss; you want to work on your own schedule in your chosen location; or other reasons for which you cannot work for someone else any longer. Generally you want to control your own destiny no matter what the impact on your lifestyle.

_____ *Other reasons:*

Your Responses and Things to Ponder

The reasons you are considering a consulting career give you some things to think about. If you rated "necessity" highest, chances are that you may not be in consulting for very long. For some, consulting is just a temporary role until they get a "real job." You may not find that you have enough funds to satisfy both your personal and business needs. This can be a strain on you, your family, and your consulting business, making it difficult to persevere. Putting your personal savings and assets on the line for the business will probably be uncomfortable for you.

If you rated "opportunity" highest, you probably also recognize how short that opportunity may be. You will want to jump quickly to exploit it, but you must first complete the planning that is required. Don't put this book down until you have completed the work through Chapter Five at least. Your business plan should ensure that you have a focus on the future and help you to determine whether demand is increasing, fading, or being taken over by others.

If you rated "personality" highest, you are competitive and will do almost anything to ensure that your consulting business survives and then thrives. Your business plan may change rapidly as you continue to see new directions you want to go in. Don't forget to tell those around you about your new directions. Although you will work hard to be successful, be sure to allow time for the personal things in your life as well.

What do you want from consulting? How will consulting support the preferred future and lifestyle you identified earlier? Summarize what you have learned about yourself and your desires for the future.

Your Goals and Consulting

Return to your lists of goals on pages 24 to 26 and rank-order all of the goals you listed. List them in priority order below. Then specify how consulting will help or hinder your ability to achieve each goal.

Rank/Goal

1.

   Helps

   Hinders

2.

   Helps

   Hinders

3.

    Helps

    Hinders

4.

    Helps

    Hinders

5.

    Helps

    Hinders

6.

    Helps

    Hinders

7.

    Helps

    Hinders

8.

    Helps

    Hinders

9.

    Helps

    Hinders

10.

    Helps

    Hinders

11.

    Helps

    Hinders

12.

    Helps

    Hinders

13.

    Helps

    Hinders

14.

    Helps

    Hinders

15.

    Helps

    Hinders

16.

    Helps

    Hinders

Examine your rank ordering and reasoning. Does consulting do more to help or hinder you to achieve your goals? How do you feel about this?

Professional, Financial, Personal, and Health Considerations

Becoming a consultant means that you will join the ranks of small business owners—entrepreneurs—as we discussed in Chapter One. Owning your own business is a major decision that will be a big change in your personal and professional life. Capture your thoughts by answering the following questions. Then discuss your responses with your spouse, significant other, or other family members who will be affected by your decision.

Professional Considerations

What is the significance of giving up your job, your title, and your affiliation with your current employer?

How will a lack of regular contact with colleagues affect your work?

How much of a risk do you take by starting your consulting business? (Although monetary risk is the first one that people think of, there are other risks.)

How long and hard are you willing to work? (If consulting will be your primary source of income, it will require a sustained level of dedication and commitment of time to become profitable.)

What if you fail? How will you deal with failure?

Financial Considerations

How much money are you willing to invest in your consulting business?

How much of your savings are you willing to invest in your business?

How will your retirement be affected if you move into consulting?

How do you feel about paying for your own dental, medical, and life insurance?

How will you react when a client does not pay on time?

How will you react if you do not meet your financial goals? (It's not unusual to work with an organization for months to line up a project, only for the deal to fall through at the last minute.)

Do you have other financial resources? If required, would it be a financial hardship to you and your family to use these resources?

Personal Considerations

How will your business affect your personal life?

How much time and energy are you willing to invest in your business, and how will this affect your personal life? (Expect to work 60 to 80 hours per week during the first year.)

How do you feel about delaying dinner, missing a Saturday trip to the zoo, or skipping a family vacation because a project took longer than you anticipated?

How do you measure and demonstrate the value of both your family and your business? How will you balance the considerations?

How will you, your family, and your friends come to an agreement about how you spend your time during the first year as you establish your business?

Health Considerations

How will owning your own business affect what you do to stay healthy?

How do you ensure that you get enough exercise now? How might that change?

How do you think your ability to find time for recreation and socializing might change?

What might you need to do differently to ensure you get enough sleep? Eat right?

Identify the Changes You Will Need to Make

Only you can determine if the time is right for you to make the switch to consulting. To help you make that decision, think about the changes you will have to make. Note that this chapter begins to explore these challenges from your personal perspective. Begin to list those challenging changes here.

I want to mention that it is not all dark and gloomy. There are ways to get around all of these, as you will discover in the upcoming chapters. For now, however, let's just stay focused on those challenges.

Professional Changes

Launching your own consulting business has professional implications. One of the surprising changes that consultants wrestle with is loneliness. Plan for this early. Who can you meet with regularly to stay connected? What other changes will you make in your lifestyle to accommodate your needs as a professional?

Financial Changes

What changes will you make to your financial situation so that it allows you to continue the lifestyle you currently have? Consider retirement savings, health and life insurance, taxes, and other out-of-pocket expenses you were not responsible for prior to owning your own business. Another option is to adjust your lifestyle and determine how you might do that. For example, if you have been the key breadwinner, might your spouse switch roles with you? Could your spouse's benefits supplement insurance needs?

Personal Changes

Without someone assigning your hours, you will have to manage your time to ensure that you take time off: nights, weekends, vacations. Do you see any changes that you will have to make to ensure a balanced lifestyle? Consider where you will work, required travel, and other things that may change your family's expectations. How else will owning your business change your personal life?

Health Changes

As a consultant, it is easy to get wrapped up in all the activities that need to be completed to start your business, find new clients, and conduct your first projects. You are about to enter the world of the entrepreneur. You may be working 60–80 hours each week to launch your business. It will be demanding. Once you are up to speed, things slow down, but in the meantime your weekends may not be free, you may have a tendency to skip exercise, and you may not eat as well as you normally do.

Most new consultants experience these, so even though I am advising you to take care, those early months will be trying. Once you get your business up and running, however, you need to focus on good health practices. Remember, one of the reasons you are starting your business is so that you can have more control of your life. How can you take control of maintaining a healthy lifestyle?

Quick Start ACTION

· ·

Create Your Personal Expense Plan

In upcoming chapters, you will create financial statements for your business. Based on what you have read in this chapter, you can see that you will want to have a solid and accurate grasp on your personal living expenses. Use the process below and the Personal Expense Plan to assist you.

1. Estimate your personal expenses for the next year. The easiest way to do this is to analyze your checkbook for the past year. Don't forget to include expenses on your credit card statements, too. Remember to think about unforeseen expenses that may occur. It's always better to plan for the worst scenario. Identify income and expenses for each month.

2. Analyze your savings, and decide exactly how much you are willing to invest in the business. Many business planners recommend that you have at least six to 12 months of living expenses in your savings account. This of course does not mean that you should plan to spend all of it before you are successful.

3. Estimate what you will withdraw from savings and how much income you believe you will receive from the business each month.

4. Summarize the data on a 12-month personal expense plan.

5. Recognize that this is only your rough estimate at this time. In upcoming chapters, you will identify start-up costs, financial targets for the business, and other financial information that will provide a more accurate picture. You will want to return to this form later. For now, however, it does give you an idea of your personal income and spending patterns.

· ·

This exercise provided a projection of your personal budget. Chapter Three leads you through several exercises that will help you anticipate your professional consulting budget and what you should pay yourself.

Personal Expense Plan

	Jan	Feb	Mar	April	May	June	July	Aug	Sept	Oct	Nov	Dec	Full Year
Expenses:													
Food													
Clothing													
Mortgage/Rent													
Utilities:													
Electricity													
Heat													
Telephone													
Entertainment													
Automobile													
Payment													
Repairs/Maintenance													
Insurance													
Medical													
School Expenses													
Child Care													
Dues													
Major Purchases													
Property Taxes													
Other Taxes													
Monthly Totals													
Income:													
Spouse/Other Income													
Cash from Business													
Savings Withdrawal													
Additional Cash Required													

Source: The New Consultant's Quick Start Guide: An Action Plan for Your First Year in Business. Copyright 2019 by Elaine Biech.

Quick Start **LISTS**

· ·

Actions I Will Take

Ideas I Have

Questions I Need to Answer

Dollars and Sense

3

In this chapter you will

- Establish a start-up budget
- Establish your pricing structure
- Calculate the revenues you will require
- Complete financial forms such as revenue projections, cash flow sheets, and expense records

Establish a Start-Up Budget

Identify everything you will need to start your consulting practice. Think in terms of furniture, equipment, supplies, occupancy costs, and setup expenses.

You may wish to go to your local office supply store and place an order for everything you think you will need. However, before you do that, consider how you could acquire the same items with a smaller outlay of cash. Look around your house. Do you have a table or chairs or bookshelves that you could borrow temporarily? Look around your neighborhood. Could you watch the ads for garage sales that might have desks or shelves? This is a good way to get the rest of your family involved in helping you. We found a fabulous solid oak desk for our receptionist that was advertised in an employee's church bulletin for $45. Watch for offices that are moving or going out of business. You will find fabulous bargains and things you never knew you needed!

Calculate how much you will need to start your business. Starting a business is an iterative process (even though it may sometimes feel as if everything has to be completed at once). Therefore, you may not be able to fill in all the blanks yet. For example, you will not explore your insurance requirements until the next chapter. Yet even though you do not know the exact cost of everything, it is important that you begin to identify what you will need and estimate the investment as accurately as possible now. Later, when you have a better idea of your insurance requirements, you will be able to estimate the cost more closely.

Identify where you will beg, borrow, and shop to fill your start-up list. Identify items and people, or companies from whom you will obtain them. While you're at it, list their telephone numbers or email addresses too. Then use the Start-Up Expenses form to organize your thoughts about what you will need and how much it should all cost.

What I Need   *Who I'll Call*

Communication/telephone equipment

Furniture

Computer, tablet, printer, and other equipment

What I Need

Office and seminar supplies

Marketing supplies

Legal support

Accounting support

Banking support

Insurance support

Who I'll Call

What I Need   *Who I'll Call*

Licenses and permits

Office space

Home office remodeling

Utilities hook-ups

Website design

Answering, printing, transcription, or graphic services

Start-Up Expenses

	Estimated Cost
Furniture	
Desk and chair	$_____
Filing cabinet	$_____
Bookcases	$_____
Table	$_____
_____	$_____
_____	$_____
Equipment	
Computer, tablet	$_____
Software: _____	
_____	
_____	$_____
Printer/Scanner	$_____
Copier	$_____
Telephone system	$_____
Business mobile phone	$_____
Postage meter or online postage services	$_____
_____	$_____
_____	$_____
Office Supplies	
Stationery	$_____
Paper: printer, specialty, other	$_____
Pens, pencils	$_____
Tape, glue, other adhesives	$_____
Scissors, rulers, miscellaneous	$_____
Seminar Supplies	
Pocket folders	$_____
Three-ring binders	$_____
_____	$_____
_____	$_____

Start-Up Expenses, Cont'd

	Estimated Cost
Marketing Supplies	
Website	$_____
Business cards	$_____
Brochures	$_____
Printed pocket folders	$_____
_____	$_____
_____	$_____
Corporate Setup Fees	
Professional fees	$_____
Legal fees (incorporation)	$_____
Business name search	$_____
Accounting fees	$_____
Banking start-up	$_____
Insurance	$_____
Licenses/permits	$_____
_____	$_____
_____	$_____
Occupancy Costs	
Rent deposit	$_____
Utilities deposit	$_____
Answering service	$_____
_____	$_____
_____	$_____
Personal Living Expenses	
Remodeling: accommodate office	$_____
Moving van	$_____
_____	$_____
_____	$_____
Additional Expenses	
_____	$_____
_____	$_____

Source: The New Consultant's Quick Start Guide: An Action Plan for Your First Year in Business. Copyright 2019 by Elaine Biech.

Put a Price on Your Head

This is the best part of this guide! You get to name your price! What will it be? $175 per hour? $250 per hour? $1,800 per day? $40,000 per project? But why would a client pay you all that money? Are you worth it? Let's begin by exploring why you may be a good investment for your clients—and worth every dollar they pay you. Then let's move on to determine what that dollar value is for you.

Five Reasons You Are a Good Investment

As technology, information, and workloads surge, so does the demand for consultants. It's all a part of the gig economy. Consulting projects have dramatically increased in recent years. All the good consultants I know have more work than they can handle. I believe there are at least three reasons behind this.

First, the need for all organizations to be more agile has increased the need to outsource more services. Whether organizations call them temps, freelancers, contractors, on-demand labor, or consultants, they are hiring more to fill the gaps and provide expertise they may not have available. They prefer this to adding highly paid permanent staff. Consultants can temporarily provide the people power to complete the work at the time it needs to be completed, allowing organizations to avoid long-term costs or commitments.

Second, the exodus of the baby boomers is still very active. In no other time in history has there been an event that has affected the workforce so keenly. Without the knowledge of this powerful group, companies struggle to sustain their current abilities. The dynamic is worldwide. Here in the United States AARP estimates that 10,000 employees reach retirement age every day. Add to that the fact that there are not enough Gen X employees to fill the jobs left behind by the boomers, and the Millennial generation is still learning. This has created the workforce shortage we are experiencing. Many organizations admit that their leaders are not as prepared as they should be to take on the roles they were meant to. This is an opportunity for consultants (some made up of the same retirees who want to work part time) to help companies fill in the gaps.

The third is related to the rapid technological changes we have come to depend on. The explosion of knowledge and the fast pace of communication make it nearly impossible for an executive team to remain completely knowledgeable about its industry, maintain focus on the innovation customers expect, and stay ahead of the competition; and the leadership team may not know instantly what to do when these factors collide. Consultants offer the knowledge, information, data, and systems to solve the puzzle.

So why would your clients pay your high prices? You may offer at least five value-added reasons.

1. **You may have the experience, expertise, and time that your clients' employees do not.** Managers are bombarded daily with new projects that require new skills and more time. In today's fast-paced, ever-changing environment, organizations have difficulty hiring enough good people just to keep up with normal, ongoing tasks. Adding the fast-paced changes to the retirement conundrum, organizations may turn to you to fill the knowledge and time gaps for the many special projects that arise. You will bring experience and expertise from past projects and other organizations.

2. **You may provide flexibility for your clients.** They may see you as someone who can be brought in for short-term projects. This is especially true if they have not planned for fast-paced changes in projects and people. You will be there when they need you and gone when they don't. Your clients will see that you will work beyond the 40-hour week to get the job done. Unlike hired staff, who require ongoing paychecks, benefits, and severance packages, consultants provide flexibility by serving their purpose and then going away.

3. **You may offer a fresh, objective point of view.** With hundreds of other projects under your belt and valuable experience in dealing with an array of situations and personalities, you will be able to provide unbiased, fresh ideas. You will bring ideas and experiences from other firms and industries. This cross-pollination is a surefire way to tap into the brainpower of many resources. Staff may be too close to the problem to see the solution. In addition, you will not be influenced by the internal politics that may prevent employees from telling the emperor he has no clothes.

4. **You will most likely be more efficient for three reasons.** First, you bring experience with similar problems and do not need to get up to speed. Second, you have the luxury of focusing solely on the assigned project or problem, unlike employees who have to complete their normal jobs while working on special projects. Third, you do not need to deal with the organization's internal politics and daily tasks: staff meetings, time and attendance records, retirement parties, emails, and other policies and procedures. You will arrive, put your head down, and get to work. Is it any wonder that a consultant can complete a project in one-fourth the time of an in-house employee?

5. **You may offer proof of honest endeavor.** When other parties are involved, you may serve as a sign that an effort is in progress. For example, during a merger or other organizational change, you might serve as an independent mediator to resolve differences. At other times, organizations may find that they are not in compliance with environmental or safety laws. You may be hired for your expertise to show that an effort has been made to correct the problem.

When it comes to the bottom line, consultants are often more cost-effective for an organization. Organizations may hire you to gain skills on an as-needed basis rather than training and educating internal staff with skills that may not be used again. You can provide the solution many organizations are looking for. You will have the skill, time, experience, and expertise to get the job done; you can offer an independent perspective and insight; you will be fair, honest, and ethical; and best of all, there will be no ongoing salary, payroll taxes, benefits, or equal employment opportunity complaints.

Now summarize the value you could add for your client:

- Do you have experience or expertise that you could implement immediately?

- Can you provide flexibility to complete short-term projects?

- Can you offer a fresh, objective point of view?

- Can you be more efficient as a consultant than as an employee?

- Do you have unique expertise that may not be found inside organizations?

Write a short paragraph responding to these questions to assure yourself that you will add value for your clients.

Calculate Required Revenue

As you determine what to charge your clients, you will need to keep two questions separate:

1. How much money do you require?

2. How much will clients be willing to pay you?

Although related, the questions present two different perspectives. If your client is willing to pay more than you need, you should not hesitate to move forward. On the other hand, if you need more money than you think a client would pay, you might want to reconsider a career as a consultant. We will be concerned primarily with uncovering the numbers in this chapter. Generally new consultants underestimate what they should charge a client. I know that I certainly did when I started out. It didn't take me too long to realize that my expertise wasn't the only reason I had more work than I could handle—I was severely undercharging! If you want a more in-depth rationale and discussion, turn to Chapter Three, "Dollars and Sense," in *The New Business of Consulting*.

How Much Money Do You Require?

You can determine how much income you will need in two ways.

First, you may calculate in detail your salary, taxes, benefits, and business expenses for one year. This will give you a very accurate calculation and a better prediction. The downside is that it is time-consuming to determine all the details.

Second, you can use what I call the "3 × Rule" (pronounced "three times rule"). This is a fast and relatively accurate estimate. The downside is that it will not provide you with the detail you may want as a start-up business.

Both are provided here. You may wish to do both and then compare the final numbers. If you are serious about moving into consulting, I recommend that you use the calculation method because this is an important step in your planning. If you are still in the exploratory stages of a consulting career, the 3 × Rule will serve you well for now.

● **The calculation method:** Most of us relate our value to the salary that we draw. Use Calculating What You Require on page 51 to identify your salary, benefits, taxes, and business expenses for one year. If it's difficult for you to identify the exact cost of your benefits because you do not have all the data at this time, you can estimate them at 33 percent of your salary. Remember when you begin to fill in the expenses that they are for one full year of operation but do not include one-time start-up expenses.

Calculating What You Require

Your Salary for One Year _____

Your Benefits
    Health insurance _____
    Life insurance _____
    Disability insurance _____
    Retirement _____
                        Total Benefits _____

Taxes
    Self-employment _____
    Social Security and Medicare _____
    State income tax _____
    City tax _____
    Personal property tax _____
                        Total Taxes _____

Business Expenses
    Accounting, banking, and legal fees _____
    Advertising and marketing _____
    Automobile expenses _____
    Books and resources _____
    Clerical support _____
    Copying and printing _____
    Donations _____
    Dues and subscriptions _____
    Entertainment _____
    Equipment leases _____
    Insurance: _____
    Casualty
    Liability
    Professional liability
    Interest and loan repayment _____
    Licenses _____
    Lodging (nonbillable) _____
    Materials (nonbillable) _____
    Meals _____
    Office supplies _____
    Postage _____
    Professional development _____
    Rent _____
    Repairs and maintenance _____
    Telephone, Internet _____
    Travel (nonbillable) _____
    Utilities _____
                        Total Business Expenses _____

Profit (consider 10% of revenue)   **Total Required** _____

Source: The New Consultant's Quick Start Guide: An Action Plan for Your First Year in Business. Copyright 2019 by Elaine Biech.

- **The 3 × Rule:** If you do not wish to spend the time identifying all your business expenses, the 3 × Rule gives a close approximation. Many consulting firms use this rule to determine how much to invoice clients for services. It also serves as a guide to know how much consultants should generate to cover their salaries. For example, consultants with a salary of $100,000 are expected to bill (and in many firms, generate, too) at least three times that amount, or $300,000. Does that seem excessive? Why is it that high? Of course, $100,000 is paid in salary. The rest is necessary to cover fringe benefits, such as insurance, FICA, unemployment taxes, workers' compensation, and vacation time; overhead, such as advertising, rent, professional development, telephone, supplies, clerical support, and management; downtime, including days when consultants are traveling, on vacation, or in training; and development and preparation time. In addition, any good business should be looking for a profit. If it is publicly held, its shareholders expect it. You will consider profit margins in Chapter Eleven. Since you are about to become a business owner, you will have these same expenses.

As a start-up company working from your home, you may consider something closer to a 2 × or 2.5 × Rule. I do caution you, however, not to cut it too closely. Your budget will be tight and you may experience cash-flow problems. For now, aim for a business revenue that is three times the salary you will draw. Figure that out here:

Your Salary $ _____ × 3 = $ _____

Determining Actual Billable Days

The next step is to identify how many billable days you expect to have in one year. The answer is not as easy as you might expect. Begin by answering the following questions:

How much time will you take off for vacations?

How much time off will you allow for illness or personal emergencies?

Do you plan to work weekends?

How much time do you need for administrative work?

How much time will you need for marketing?

How much other down time do you expect to encounter?

Once you've answered these questions, fill in the following chart to determine your actual billable days.

Days in a Year	365
Weekend Days	−104
	=261
Time Off	
Vacation, personal (5 to 15 days per year)	− _____
Holidays (6 to 12 days per year)	= _____
	= _____
Marketing (1 to 2 days per week)	− _____
Administrative (2 to 4 days per month)	= _____
	= _____
Down time (15 to 30 percent)	− _____
Days you expect to work	_____

Source: The New Consultant's Quick Start Guide: An Action Plan for Your First Year in Business. Copyright 2019 by Elaine Biech.

Calculating a Daily Fee

Now let's put the two figures together. Divide what you require by the number of days you expect to work to identify your daily fee. If you expect to charge by the hour, divide that by eight.

What you require/Days you expect to work = Daily Fee

$_____ / _____ days = $_____ per day

Calculating an Hourly Fee

Daily Fee / 8 Hours = Hourly Fee

_____ / 8 Hours = $_____ per hour

How do you feel about the amount you have identified?

How Much Will Clients Pay?

Ultimately the client determines acceptable fee ranges. The factors that determine how much a client will pay fall into two categories. The first is the client: the industry, the size, location, demand, and reliance on the consultant in the past. The second is the consultant: the level of expertise, time in the consulting field, stature in the profession, name recognition, and area of expertise. I've worked with consultants who have charged as little as $200 per day and with those who charge as much as $75,000 for a one-hour speech.

To determine whether you will charge at the high end or the low end, compare the following pairs of descriptions. Place an X in either the left or right column next to the one that more closely describes you and your potential clients. This is certainly not a foolproof way to determine what you will charge. It does, however, give you more information and demonstrates why a wide variation in consultants' pricing exists.

My Consulting

___ Expertise in high demand	___ Minimal demand for expertise
___ A specialized niche	___ Lots of competition
___ More than 20 years in industry	___ Less than 10 years in industry
___ High name recognition	___ Little name recognition
___ Area of specialty rare	___ Specialty readily available
___ Offer customized solution	___ Offer content with minor tailoring
___ My confidence level is high	___ I'm just getting started
___ Fills a gap in the workforce	___ Skills/knowledge easily accessible
___ Published work is well known	___ No published work

My Clients

—— High-operating-margin industry	—— Low-operating-margin industry
—— For-profit organizations	—— Nonprofit organizations or government
—— Large companies	—— Small companies
—— Large city	—— Small town
—— U.S. Coast locations	—— U.S. Midwest
—— High use of consultants	—— Minimal use of consultants
—— Urgent, burning issues	—— Not time-sensitive
Totals ——	——————

Total the Xs in each column. The more Xs you have in the left column, the higher rate you will be able to charge.

Before Moving On

Before you finalize your fee, I'd like to describe the various ways that consultants charge, and acknowledge that some get very testy about the *right* way to charge. In my mind, there is no one right way. It depends on where you are in your career. And, since you are likely starting out, I presented hourly and daily fees as the easiest way that consultants can define what they charge to their clients. You need a place to start. What are the various ways?

- **Hourly fees.** This pricing structure gets the most grief, because it is seen as limiting your options. Even so, there may be times when an hourly fee is the best way. Jenn Labin, of TERP associates, doesn't usually charge by the hour, but she defines several times when an hourly fee works: when a significant amount of ramp-up time is necessary, when you aren't confident in the process or technology, and if the scope isn't stable. Take care when billing this way. Your hourly rate could be so high that no one would see the value.

- **Daily fees.** This is the calculation we just worked through and receives almost as much grief as hourly rates. I still think it is a good place to start because it gives you a perspective of how to value yourself. Don't forget that your daily rate should be charged for design time, as well as time on-site.

Some consultants charge a daily rate high enough to include preparation and design time. Be sure your clients know this.

- **Project rate.** I tend to charge a project rate. I define a fixed amount up front and then establish payment around milestones or a timeline. It can be the easiest to transition into, now that you have an approximate amount you would charge on a daily basis. Of course, estimating the time may be tricky at first. Be sure your proposal is clear about deliverables up front and be cautious about scope creep!

- **Retainer basis.** This gives you a set monthly fee in which you agree to be available every month for an agreed-upon number of hours. The advantage is a regular income. The drawback is that clients often have clauses in the contract preventing you from working with their competitors. If you focus on one industry, this may limit your income. Retainers are hard to sell to clients when you are just starting out—unless they are familiar with your work.

- **Value-based fees.** This method may be the most complex, though it has many strong advocates. You have to confidently explain to your client how you determine the amount. It is based on you receiving a percent of the savings or additional profit you create for your clients based on the project. Generally, this method only works when you are the only one who is qualified to complete the project.

Fill Out Financial Forms

Although it might seem early in the process to begin to think in terms of a budget and cash-flow projections, the truth is that it can never be too early to project what it will take to manage the finances of your business. The next three forms will help you do that. One of the first things you will want to do is select an accountant. Ask your accountant to recommend the financial software that will be best for your needs and compatible with your accountant's software. Your software is likely to produce these same or similar forms. The forms are posted here so that you can begin to plan how you will manage the financial aspect of your business.

The Budget Format provides a way for you to list all expenses you expect for the year. The First-Year Cash-Flow Projection form will help you organize the flow of money coming in and going out the first year. Cash flow is critical and is often a key reason that businesses fail: they can't pay their bills. This happens because there is a delay between expenses you incur for a project and the income you will receive from it.

Setting Your Fee

Check the competition. Before moving forward, check your market area for services similar to yours and identify what they are charging. For example, a local mental health clinic may offer a stress-management class for $25. Your local community college may offer on-site support for identifying corporate computer needs at $75 per hour. A local training, consulting, or facilitation association chapter may offer facilitation as a community service. If any of these is similar to what you offer, you may have a difficult time convincing companies to pay $1,500 per day for your services—even if you do customize the materials for them. Start by making a few telephone calls to members of your network. Jot down any information you learn below.

And the Number Is …

You've calculated, contemplated, researched, and studied. It's time to put the figure on paper.

The fee I will charge clients is:

$_____ per _____

Budget Format

Net Salary for One Year _____

Benefits

    Health insurance _____

    Life insurance _____

    Disability insurance _____

    Retirement _____

                                  Total Benefits _____

Taxes

    Self-employment _____

    Social Security and Medicare _____

    State income tax _____

    City tax _____

    Personal property tax _____

                                  Total Taxes _____

Business Expenses

    Accounting, banking, legal fees _____

    Advertising and marketing _____

    Automobile expenses _____

    Books and resources _____

    Clerical support _____

    Copying and printing _____

    Donations _____

    Dues and subscriptions _____

    Entertainment _____

    Equipment leases _____

    Insurance _____

    Interest and loan repayments _____

    Licenses _____

    Lodging (nonbillable) _____

    Materials (nonbillable) _____

    Meals _____

    Office supplies _____

    Postage _____

    Professional development _____

    Rent _____

    Repairs and maintenance _____

    Salaries (employees) _____

    Seminar expenses _____

    Telephone _____

    Travel (nonbillable) _____

    Utilities _____

                                  Total Business Expenses _____

                                  Profit _____

                                  Total Required for One Year _____

Source: The New Consultant's Quick Start Guide: An Action Plan for Your First Year in Business. Copyright 2019 by Elaine Biech.

First-Year Cash-Flow Projection

	Jan	Feb	March	April	May	June	July	Aug	Sept	Oct	Nov	Dec
Revenue												
Total Revenue												
Expenses												
Accounting/banking/legal												
Advertising/marketing												
Automobile												
Benefits												
Books/resources												
Clerical support												
Copying/printing												
Donations												
Dues/subscriptions												
Entertainment												
Equipment leases												
Insurance												
Interest												
Licenses												
Lodging												
Materials												
Meals												
Office supplies												
Postage												
Professional development												
Rent												
Repairs/maintenance												
Salaries												
Seminar expenses												
Taxes												
Telephone												
Travel												
Utilities												
Total Expenses												
Monthly Cash Flow												
Cumulative Cash Flow												

Source: The New Consultant's Quick Start Guide: An Action Plan for Your First Year in Business. Copyright 2019 by Elaine Biech

Three-Year Cash Flow Projection

	Year 1	Year 2	Year 3
Total Revenue	————	————	————
Expenses:			
Salaries	————	————	————
Benefits	————	————	————
Taxes	————	————	————
Marketing	————	————	————
Administrative/Overhead	————	————	————
Total Expenses	————	————	————
5 Percent Inflation	no*	————	————
Expenses + Inflation	no*	————	————
Projection	————	————	————
Revenue – Adjusted Expenses			
After Inflation	————	————	————

*No inflation is added the first year.
Source: The New Consultant's Quick Start Guide: An Action Plan for Your First Year in Business. © Elaine Biech.

For example, you may complete a project during the month of May, incurring copying, travel, and overhead costs, and you bill the client for your work on June 1. It may take three to five days for your invoice to reach the client's accounts payable department. Most companies wait until the last minute to pay their bills. (This helps their cash flow situation and allows them to collect interest as long as possible—something you should do as well.) You may not receive a check for your work until the middle of July. And that's the positive scenario. Your invoice could be lost in the mail or in the client's system. The check could get lost on its way to you. In the meantime, you have those expenses incurred in May to pay. Add other projects to this scenario and you see how quickly the problem can compound.

As you complete your cash-flow projections, I recommend that you think practically and plan generously so you are less likely to be caught in a cash-flow crunch.

The Three-Year Cash-Flow Projection form gives you the same perspective but for a longer period of time. It is also more general. Think three years out. How profitable will you be by then?

So What's It Take to Get Off the Ground?

Okay, we know you just want to get started, find a place to hang out, get your first gig, and call yourself a consultant. What's it gonna take?

What Will It Cost?

Running a business means that you must pay your bills every month. So after all the numbers we've just run through, what's it really going to take to get started? How much money will you need?

The total cost is actually a combination of two things. The first is your start-up costs. These are one-time costs to open your business, and you won't encounter many of them again. Some, like insurance, will be due on a quarterly or semiannual basis. Others, like the desk you borrowed from Aunt June and the scratch-and-dent bargain you picked up at the surplus store, will not cost anything again until you replace them.

Where Will I Find the Money?

Some financial advisers recommend that you have six months' living expenses saved. Others recommend a full year. It really depends on you and whether you have a supplemented income or whether you can tighten your belt. You can use your estimated living expenses from Chapter Two to judge whether you have sufficient savings. It goes beyond just your living expenses. You need to ensure that your business has enough operating capital—enough cash on hand to make it through the initial period as you sell your services and begin to receive revenue.

If you have decided to move forward and do not have all the money you need, you will spend time examining your dilemma in Chapter Six. Now let's depart from the financial discussions and identify other aspects of starting your business in the next chapter.

Quick Start LISTS

Actions I Will Take

Ideas I Have

Questions I Need to Answer

Taking Care of Business $\blacktriangleright$ **4**

In this chapter you will

- Name your business
- Learn how to find the best accountant and attorney
- Determine the best business structure
- Explore your banking and insurance needs
- Check zoning laws, licenses, and taxes for which you will be responsible
- File legal documentation
- Create a to-do list to organize all that needs to be completed to start your business

Getting Started

You've probably figured out by now that there are many tasks to starting a business and getting off the ground. If you have been working through the tasks along the way, you have completed a great deal of the preliminary work that will prepare you for this chapter. You will find a to-do list at the end of this chapter that will remind you of everything that needs to be completed at this stage. Let's begin by determining what you want to call your consulting business.

What's in a Name?

What's in a name? Actually quite a bit. The name you select for your business will have strong implications for how your clients view you and your business. Your business name is the first image you present to your clients.

Selecting your business name requires two important considerations. First, you want to select a name that is easy to remember so your clients will remember to call you. Second, select a name that is professional and establishes your image. If you can also select a name that says what you do, all the better. But it goes beyond that. What will your clients think of when they see or hear your business name? For example, you might choose to use your name. The advantage of "Joe Bloomer Consulting" is that it tells potential clients who you are and the nature of your business. The drawback is that it limits your clients' perception of your business to one person. Joe may have 10 people working for him, but the name will prevent that information from readily surfacing.

What is your vision for the future of your consulting business? Will you have employees? Associates? Partners? Your name should allow for your future growth or challenge. Many consultants use "Joe Bloomer and Associates" or "The Bloomer Group," even though Joe may be starting out on his own. That way, they are prepared for adding others as they grow the business.

The drawback of using your name in any configuration is that you identify yourself as the head person, and your colleagues may see this negatively because they may want to join you in your consulting business. But if you have strong name recognition, such as "The Ken Blanchard Companies," using your name can be an advantage to both finding clients and hiring people.

Some consultants choose the name of their business's location as a name. Some names may sound great, but you will need to determine whether they also might be limiting. "The Northwest Group" sounds impressive and conjures up great graphics, but will companies in the Midwest and the Southeast in the United States consider hiring you? And consider this one: "Herrmann International" is the ultimate in not limiting yourself to one locale. If you plan to offer services throughout the world you could include descriptors such as global, international, worldwide, or others.

Select a name that exudes a professional image and, if possible, tells the client what you do. "Bloomer Executive Coaching" or "Team Solutions" tells potential clients what you do. At a minimum, your company name should not confuse clients. A word of caution: be careful that your name doesn't limit the services you may want to offer in the future. For example, "Bloomer Executive Coaching" may be limiting if Joe wants to add strategic planning to what he offers next year.

Take care that you do not get too cute with a name choice so that your consulting business sounds amateurish. If your name is Mark Fish, for example, "Fish Food for Thought" might be a great name for an aquarium business, but not for a consulting business. You want to be taken seriously.

Your goal is to make it easy for clients to select you by name the first time and to remember you by name forever after. You will build up name recognition the longer you consult. Therefore, select something that you will be able to live with for a long time. You may also want to think about the graphics that could support your name. Although it took the marketing agency nine months to convince me to use waves with my corporate name, "ebb," it has proven to be the right choice. Clients relate the visual to the name.

You may also want to consider how you intend to brand your business. Will you be a loud and in-their-face kind of consultant? Or will you be formal and strong? Or maybe fun and creative? You may think it is a bit early to consider this now, but your corporate name will help tell your story and brand your services. The name is an important aspect of marketing your services.

Think also about the images that come to mind with the names you have chosen. How might they appear on all types of media you may choose in the future: stationery, business cards, website, journal ad, maybe even a billboard.

If your business name is anything besides your own, you are required to register it with the secretary of state's office in the state where you intend to do business. In addition, if you use any name in addition to the one you've chosen, you must file a Certificate of Trade Name or a "doing business as" (DBA) certificate. For example, your corporation may be Greene Ventures, Inc., and you may name your consulting practice Corporate Computer Consulting. This practice allows you to do business in states where someone else is already known as Greene Ventures, Inc. In addition, this practice allows you to incorporate once and have flexibility for various new start-ups. Contact your local city or state officials for more information.

Quick · · · · · · · · · ▶ TIP

If you are having difficulty deciding on a name or even thinking of some creative possibilities, try one of these name-generating options: www.shopify.com, www.namelix.com, www.businessnamegenerator.com, or many others

> *(Cont'd)*
>
> online. You might also go to www.entrepreneurs.about.com, a website that describes a process for naming a business. Once you get to the site, click on "Starting a Business." The website also offers other services to entrepreneurs. Once you have selected a couple of possible names, use your favorite search engine to conduct a quick check to determine whether the name is being used in any other way. Be sure the name is easy to say and spell. Say it aloud. Does it sound positive?

And if you wish to trademark your name, you will need your attorney's assistance.

List eight possible names here for your business. Then try them out on colleagues to get feedback. What do your colleagues say about each?

1.

2.

3.

4.

5.

6.

7.

8.

Choose the Right Name

Selecting the right name can be one of the most powerful marketing decisions you will make as you start your business. I didn't think through all the ramifications of a company name, but I got lucky. I wanted the name to send a quiet message of professionalism and uniqueness. I achieved it by using all lowercase letters and no punctuation. To extend that image, I printed my marketing materials using gray type on a lighter gray paper. People did not always remember the specific name, ebb associates inc, but they remembered the impression and might say something like, "Remember that company with the three small letters?" I was lucky with my choice.

Choosing the right name can provide a powerful foundation for everything else you do. Don't try to make it do everything. What are you trying to accomplish with your name? Prioritize these messages that you want your business name to send. Then compare them to the options you have listed so far.

☐ Be memorable

☐ Help you stand apart from your competition

☐ Deliver a best-of-brand perspective

☐ Clarify a unique positioning platform

☐ Exude professionalism

☐ Interject fun or excitement

☐ Be its own marketing lever

☐ Define what you do

☐ Be evocative

☐ Convey a benefit

Hire the Best Accountant and Attorney

You will need to find an accountant and an attorney immediately. You may be thinking that it is too early for an accountant—you haven't made any money yet! An accountant is necessary at this time to provide good advice for the many decisions you will be making. An attorney will also help you start on the right foot and let you know what records you should keep.

You will find a good accountant the same way you find good restaurants, dry cleaners, and barbers: networking. Ask other businesspeople, especially other consultants, whom they use. Identify the qualities you are looking for so that you can describe your ideal accountant. In the best case, you will find someone who has experience with small consulting start-ups.

Interview several accountants before you select the one with whom you will work. This is one of the most important relationships in your business. You will work with your accountant at least once a month.

What are you looking for in an accountant?

- Keeps you informed of new tax laws?
- Keeps you informed of retirement law changes?
- Challenges you?
- Takes risks or is risk averse?

What services do you want your accountant to provide?

- Tax preparation?
- Monthly record keeping?
- Monthly statement generation?
- Payroll services?

When I found a great accountant, I asked her to recommend an attorney. This was the start of my team. You will experience more value if your accountant and your attorney already collaborate on other business.

Even with a recommendation from your accountant, spend time interviewing the attorney. You want to feel comfortable that the person will meet your needs. You might ask these questions in your interview:

- What experience have you had with consulting firms?

- How have you worked with my accountant in the past?

- How can we best work together?

- How do you charge for the work you do: flat fee or hourly rate?

- Can you provide some examples of flat fee rates for services I might use?

- If you charge an hourly rate, what is that rate?

- What determines whether someone else in the firm will work with me?

- What other costs are involved?

- How can you be reached in times of emergency (through office staff or at home)?

- Who can you provide as references?

After your interview, reflect on these questions:

- How comfortable did you feel with the attorney?

- Was the attorney interested in you?

- Did you understand everything the attorney told you?

- Did the attorney use words you understood and define those you didn't?

- Did the attorney's answers meet your needs?

- Do you feel that this attorney will have your best interests in mind?

- Will you feel comfortable calling the attorney with questions?

After you have decided on an accountant and an attorney, the first thing they will do for you is to help you decide on the best business structure for your consulting business.

Quick Start **ACTION**

- -

Find an Accountant and Attorney

Identify three possible accountants or attorneys now (or both):

Accountants

1.

2.

3.

Attorneys

1.

2.

3.

Begin to schedule interviews with these people over the next couple of weeks.

- -

Determine Your Business Structure

The next step is to determine the best business structure for your situation. Once you have found an accountant and an attorney, take your plans to them and ask for their advice. Determining a business structure may be confusing; however, in the United States, there are basically only four general types:

- Sole proprietorships

- Partnerships

- Corporations (C and S)

- Limited liability partnerships or companies

If you are forming your consulting business outside the United States, seek advice from someone who understands the laws regarding business structures in that country. Also, be aware that laws are different from state to state. If you plan to do business outside your state, be sure to discuss this with your accountant and attorney.

Sole Proprietorship

A sole proprietorship is the simplest business structure. It is not a separate legal entity from the owner, and usually your Social Security number serves as your company's federal taxpayer identification number. There is no registration requirement other than an assumed name filing if you want to do business in another state or under a different name.

Partnerships

Partnerships are formed when two or more people form a business entity. Each general partner has an equal voice in managing the business, which is identified by a federal employer identification number (FEIN). The traditional partnership is known as a *general partnership*. A *limited partnership* has limited partners in addition to the general partners. Limited partners share in the profit and loss, have limited rights to managing the business, and have limited liability.

Corporations

Corporations can be formed as C corporations or as subchapter-S corporations. All corporations are separate and distinct legal entities, and ownership interests can be transferred. To form a corporation, you must file articles of incorporation, receive a charter issued by a state, create bylaws, and fulfill other state requirements. Subchapter-S corporations have the distinct advantage of not being double-taxed as a C corporation is, which means that the owners pay taxes as a corporation and again as individuals. A subchapter-S corporation is often referred to as an S corp.

Limited Liability Structures

Limited liability companies (LLCs) and limited liability partnerships (LLPs) have a corporate look but qualify for other partnership or corporate tax status. As more relaxed entities, they combine limited liability protection without all the corporate formalities.

The Comparison of Basic Business Entities chart provides you with a comparison of characteristics of all these business structures. Examine it before visiting your accountant or attorney.

The Business Structure That's Best for You

Your attorney and accountant will help you determine the business structure that's best for you. Complete the Business Entity Selection Worksheet here, and take your responses to them. The answers to these questions will also prepare you to develop your business plan in Chapter Five. As you and your professionals compare the different business structures, consider these issues:

- Cost of forming
- Process for filing
- Cost to maintain and operate the entity
- Liability risks
- Formalities to operate, such as requirements to hold annual meetings or submit meeting minutes to the state in which you incorporate
- Ability to transfer ownership
- Length of time you expect your business to exist
- Amount of privacy you require

Comparison of Basic Business Entities

Entity	Owner Liability	Participation in Management	Ownership	Formation Requirements	Name
Sole Proprietor	No limits.	No restrictions.	One.	None. File assumed name if doing business in another state or under different name.	No special requirements.
General Partnership	No limits.	No restrictions.	At least two partners.	Partnership agreement (may be oral) and file assumed name certificate.	No special requirements.
Limited Partnership	No limits for general partners. Limited for limited partners.	Restrictions for limited partners	At least one general partner and one limited partner.	Partnership agreement (may be oral) and file certificate with Secretary of State.	Must have "Limited Partnership," "Ltd.," "Limited," or "L.P." in title.
Limited Liability Company	All members have limited liability for company debts.	No restrictions. ("Managing" members make decisions.)	One or more members. (Some states may require at least two members.)	File Articles of Organization and adopt regulations.	Must have "Limited Liability Company," "LLC," or "LC" in title. ("Limited" and "Company" may be abbreviated.)

Comparison of Basic Business Entities Con't

Entity	Owner Liability	Participation in Management	Ownership	Formation Requirements	Name
S Corporation	Limited liability for all shareholders.	No restrictions. (Shareholders elect directors to make decisions. Directors appoint officers for daily decisions.)	One to 75 shareholders.	File Articles of Incorporation, adopt bylaws, and file "S" election tax form with IRS.	Must have "Corporation," "Incorporated," "Company," or abbreviation of these in title.
C Corporation	Limited liability for all shareholders.	No restrictions. (Shareholders elect directors to make decisions. Directors appoint officers for daily decisions.)	One or more shareholders.	File Articles of Incorporation and adopt bylaws.	Must have some form of "Corporation," "Incorporated," "Company," or abbreviation of these in title

Source: E. Biech and L. Byars Swindling, *The Consultant's Legal Guide* (San Francisco: Jossey-Bass/Pfeiffer, 2000).

Business Entity Selection Worksheet

Ask yourself these questions as you decide on the best business entity for you. Review the answers with your attorney and accountant to help make your structure decisions.

What type of business are you creating?

What services and/or products will you offer?

How will you distribute those services and/or products?

Where will the business operations be located?

Who will own this business?

How much of the business will each person own?

Who will manage the business, and what role will each person play?

What is your financial plan?

How much capital will you require? When? In what form?

What are your start-up costs?

What are your income projections?

How will profits and losses be allocated?

What are the financial resources of the owners?

What are the assets of the business?

What action will you take if you are not meeting your financial goals?

Who is your competition?

What is your marketing strategy?

Where is your customer base located?

How long do you plan to be in business?

Do you plan to sell the business someday?

Will you want to sell part of the business to raise money? (Stock or membership interest?)

Do you plan to transfer the business to a family member?

Do you have any estate planning issues regarding the business?

Are there any special tax issues regarding your type of business?

Are there any special laws or regulatory constraints on your type of business or on the owners?

What is your potential exposure to risks and liabilities?

What is your potential risk in addition to the equity invested in the business?

How will you keep track of the legal requirements or formalities of your business entity?

What happens on death, disability, retirement, or departure of a principal?

Finalize Your Decision About Structure

I suggest that you consider forming an LLC or an S corp to ensure that you have the kind of liability protection you will need.

The business structure for _____ (name) will be _____. The key reasons are:

Explore Your Banking and Insurance Needs

A banker and good insurance providers will also be important members of your business team.

Bank on Good Advice

Establish a separate bank account for your business from the start. Using your personal checking account may seem easier, but for good record keeping, it is wise to separate the accounts. Besides, the law requires it of partnerships and corporations. You will also be required to file a Schedule C with your income tax return, and a separate bank account makes this easier. Commingled business and personal funds may raise tax issues and liability issues for you later. Don't take a chance. Keep personal finances and business finances separate. Some people use separate banks to avoid confusion or errors.

Your banking needs may not seem critical initially, but you will find that a good banker can become a close and valuable partner. How do you select one? Ask your accountant and your attorney for recommendations. If the members of your support team work together, it will often be more helpful to you. You can also ask other businesspeople for suggestions.

Be certain that each bank is financially sound, follows established commercial banking practices, and has a good customer service reputation. Especially important to you is their start-up business support and small-business advocacy. Interview each potential banker about the bank's services and methods of operation. You might begin with these questions:

- Is the bank federally insured?
- Does it offer the services you need today:

- Loans in the amount you anticipate?

- Checking accounts?

- Money market accounts?

- Certificate of deposit accounts?

- Advisory services?

- Safe-deposit box?

- Wire transfer?

- Electronic banking?

- Direct deposit?

- Night drop?

- Trust services? Retirement support?

- What cybersecurity process do they have in place? What experience have they had with consulting firms?

- If you plan to work internationally, can the bank handle foreign currencies?

- What kind of fees will you pay for your checking account? Is it free with a minimum balance?

- How soon will you need to order checks? How much will they cost?

- Can you easily bank by computer?

- How can you access your account information?

- Is ATM access readily available?

- How do you qualify for a revolving line of credit and for what amount?

- What business advice does the bank provide and in what format, such as in brochures, by phone, or through seminars?

- What networking capabilities does the bank have? Can it put you in touch with suppliers, potential clients, or other business owners?

- How well did you connect with the people you interviewed? How comfortable will you be discussing your financial needs with them in the future?

- What needs does the bank think you might anticipate in the future that you did not ask about?

Be sure to discuss possible financing for your consulting business. The estimates you prepared of personal income and expenses in Chapter Two should give you an idea of when you might need financing. It's probably best to wait to request specific financing until you have completed your business plan in Chapter Five and your transition plan in Chapter Six. Nevertheless, it's good to test the waters with your bank now. How open and receptive do the people you are consulting with seem about financing, and what options do they suggest?

Insure Your Success

Insurance is a way to transfer some of the risk to another entity. For a consultant starting out, several types of insurance coverage are essential, and others might be nice to have. A word of caution: Don't skimp on insurance. It is worth the peace of mind to be well covered.

Review all of your insurance needs with a broker you trust. This does not mean, however, that you should not shop around for the best coverage at the lowest price. I recently purchased a commercial building and wanted to use the insurance agent I already had because we had built a relationship. When I went out for bids on the new property, I was able to get more coverage for almost $600 less with another reputable agency. I took the figure back to my agent, who just shook her head and said she could not match it. I still asked her to look over the new policy and to reassure me that the company was reputable.

If you have an insurance agent, start there, though recognize that all agents do not cover all insurance needs. If you don't currently have an insurance agent interview potential insurance agents and brokers. Generally an agent works for one company and a broker represents multiple companies. Consider these questions:

- How many kinds of insurance do you represent?

- How many insurance companies do you represent?

- What kinds of policies have you written for consultants?

- What references can you provide from other consultants?

- What insurance coverage do you think I need?

- What are the features of the policies you recommend?

- What is the rating for the insurance companies you propose to handle my needs?

What kind of insurance might you need? Most employees take for granted the insurance provided to them by their employers: health, life, disability, business liability, and others. As you move to self-employed status, you are probably focused on health insurance for yourself and your family. Although health insurance is certainly critical, don't forget about other essential insurance. Consider coverage for some or all of these kinds of insurance:

- *Health.* If you work for a company of 20 or more employees, you qualify for COBRA (Consolidated Omnibus Budget Reconciliation Act) coverage, which provides you the opportunity to continue with the company's group health insurance plan for 18 months after leaving the company. You will pay the premiums yourself, but it is usually less expensive than the individual policy you will eventually use. Use this temporarily, and have your permanent insurance in place six to eight weeks before COBRA expires. You have these options for permanent health insurance: your professional association may offer group plans or discounts; if your spouse works, you might be added to your spouse's policy; or you can obtain individual policies through agencies.
- *Disability.* These benefits are paid if you cannot work. Although many people often overlook this insurance, as a self-employed consultant, you cannot afford to ignore disability insurance.
- *Casualty.* Sometimes called property insurance, it covers damage, destruction, or theft of property.
- *Liability.* This coverage protects you if someone is hurt on your property. You should consider coverage of at least $5 million.
- *Professional liability.* This protects you from claims by clients you caused injury or harm to (including financial loss) due to mistakes in the service you provided. Although it can be expensive and difficult to locate, you should at least consider it. Consultants can buy protection for errors and omissions (E&O), a type of professional liability, through a professional or trade association. For example, the International Computer Consultants Association offers this coverage to its members.
- *Workers' compensation.* This is regulated and standardized by state governments, and you will most likely purchase it from a broker. As a sole proprietor, you may exclude yourself from this coverage, but you are responsible for coverage for all employees and sometimes subcontractors you may employ.

Depending on your situation, there are other forms of coverage you might consider as well: business interruption, crime, rent, group health, retirement income, and key-man insurance. It is best to discuss your requirements with your insurance broker.

Use the following list to discuss your insurance needs with an insurance agent or broker. Even if you have coverage, you will want to explain your intentions for consulting. For example, if you intend to work from your home and you have a homeowner's policy, it may not cover injuries to someone visiting for business purposes or the full value of business equipment you have in your home. Your auto insurance may not cover you if you use your car for business purposes.

My Business Insurance Needs

Type of Insurance	Recommended Coverage and Limits	Cost
Automobile		
Business interruption		
Casualty		
Crime		
Disability		
Errors and omissions		
Health		
Liability		
Professional liability		
Rent		
Workers' compensation		
Other		

Quick · · · · · · · · · · ▶ TIP

Want to read more about insurance for small businesses before meeting with a broker? Check the Insurance Information Institute's website for insuring a small business at http://www.iii.org/smallbusiness/intro/, where you will find an excellent glossary and other information about all the various insurances to consider.

Check Local Zoning Laws, Licenses, and Taxes

Your accountant and attorney will probably remind you of your obligations as a business owner, but it is still your responsibility to ensure that you do everything required.

Zoning laws are usually regulated by the municipality in which you intend to operate. If you are considering an office in your home, check out pertinent zoning laws. Local zoning restrictions might prevent you from having employees, posting signs, or operating certain types of businesses from your home.

Every city is different; therefore, call about the zoning ordinances that cover your situation. Unfortunately, the name of the office will be different in every city as well. It may be called the zoning board, building code, code compliance, or something else. A few calls should eventually get you to the right person. Once that happens, ask for the specific zoning ordinances that cover your situation. If the person says there is no problem, keep a record of your discussion and the name of the person who provided this information.

If there is a restriction that prevents you from having a consulting practice in your home, you can always ask for a variance—an alteration that grants a change for one person. For example, if you are planning to hire a part-time clerical person and the zoning laws prohibit you from employing nonfamily members in your home, you could file a formal application for a variance with your local government. Be sure to check on all the procedures before you make your request:

- Where do you make your application?

- Do you need your neighbors' approval?

- Do you need their approval in writing?

- Do you need to attend the board meeting in person?

- Do you need architectural drawings?

Follow the procedures. Not doing so may result in a delay, and in some municipalities the zoning board may meet as infrequently as every six months.

During the same time you are checking on zoning laws, determine whether your city or state requires you to have a business license for your consulting practice.

Finally, check on taxes. Some large cities require that you pay a city tax on your gross income. It is often quite small—as little as 0.5 percent. In some cases, if you do business in two cities and one does not charge a city tax, the second one might lay claim to all your work. Your accountant will assist you with these questions and calculate how much tax you owe.

File Legal Documentation

Once you've determined the best structure for your business, file documentation to legally register it. Your attorney will assist you with filing the documentation required.

Also, request your federal employer identification number (EIN). You will need this number—if you have chosen anything except a sole proprietorship—to file tax returns, open a business bank account, deposit employment taxes (if you have employees), and establish a company retirement plan.

Your accountant or attorney may obtain your EIN for you. If you need to do it, however, it is easy to do online. After you complete the documentation, you will have the actual number before you can pour a cup of coffee. Obtain your EIN on line at www.irs.gov/businesses/small-businesses-self-employed. Follow the link to Employer ID Numbers (EIN).

You may also need a state employer identification number. Check with your state's Department of Revenue (or Taxation) and Department of Labor for the requirements. If you live outside the United States, you will need to contact your appropriate government agencies. Again, your accountant or attorney will help.

Once you've worked through all the activities in this chapter, your consulting business should feel closer to reality. Putting your business plan together in the next chapter will firm up that reality even more.

Quick Start ACTION

. . . .

Your First To-Do List

Okay. You've read through (and probably written in) this book for four chapters. It is time you took some action—that is, if you haven't already! In Chapter Five, you will begin to write a business plan. It will be easier if you have completed several tasks prior to that time. Here's the beginning of your first to-do list. If you have already completed items on the list, good for you! Check them off. It is time to turn your thinking, planning, and considering into action. Note that the worksheets in the first four chapters help you complete the actions. Be sure to add others that are unique to your needs.

My To-Do List

☐ _Meet with a consultant._

☐ _Assess my skills._

☐ _Identify the focus of my consulting practice._

☐ _Talk to my family about what I am thinking._

☐ _Meet with several colleagues to get their thoughts._

☐ _Identify a mentor._

☐ _Complete my budget figures._

☐ _Determine my financial requirements (budget) and pricing structure._

☐ _Identify my start-up costs._

☐ _Decide (perhaps temporarily) what I intend to charge clients._

☐ _Name my company._

☐ _Begin an URL search for my website._

☐ _Start creatively thinking about my logo, business cards, and other stationery needs._

☐ _Begin networking with others to share my plans._

☐ _Decide on the online presence I'd like._

☐ _Select and meet with an accountant._

☐ _Select a banker, attorney, and insurance broker._

☐ _Determine my business structure._

☐ _Determine my insurance needs_

☐ _Arrange for financing (or set aside capital for a worst-case scenario)._

☐ _File documentation to legally register my business._

☐ _Check on zoning laws, licenses, and taxes._

☐ _Select a location for my office._

Quick Start LISTS

Actions I Will Take

Ideas I Have

Questions I Need to Answer

Your Business Plan

5

In this chapter you will

- Develop your business plan
- Determine how you will use your business plan

Are Business Plans Really Necessary?

Business plans are critical. Without them, you may end up in a place you didn't intend to be. I know, because it happened to me. When I started, I fully intended to be a solopreneur, working without additional staff. I didn't think I needed a business plan for that. Besides, there was too much to do! I began marketing with gusto and soon had too much work to finish myself, so I hired another consultant. Of course, I realized that I would need to go after larger contracts to pay both our salaries, but the added marketing intensity led to more work than the two of us could handle, so we invested more of our time in marketing, and, yes, you guessed it, we had too much work to meet our clients' needs, and so . . . yes, I hired another consultant, which required more support staff. I accidentally built a company. Good or bad? Neither. It just wasn't what I had planned. I would not have been in that predicament if I'd had a well-thought-out business plan.

A business plan is a document that describes your consulting business and where you want it to go in the future. Many new consultants are impatient to get started with the real work of consulting, so planning at this time may seem to be a waste of time when there is so much else to do. Planning may seem less critical than earning money when there is no income yet. Planning may not seem very action-oriented and, quite frankly, you may find it boring! Fewer than half of all new consulting businesses take the time to write a business plan.

Nevertheless, a business plan is a critical document. Let's remind ourselves of the value of writing a business plan from the perspective of both the process and the result:

The Process

- Encourages you to think strategically

- Forces you to face difficult issues and concerns

- Provides you with a realistic view of actions that require your attention

- Compels you to think about all key aspects of the business (marketing, financial, product or service)

- Stimulates new ideas

- Creates time for you to organize all of your ideas in one place

The Result

- Maintains your focus

- Delineates the strengths and weaknesses of your decisions

- Communicates your vision and expectations for the future

- Provides a presentation package to raise money

- Provides a guide for making decisions about the business

- Becomes a tool for measuring progress

- Creates a road map for the future

- Serves as a reference document

Still not convinced that writing a business plan is a necessity? Perhaps you should identify why you are avoiding the task. Answer the following questions to help you understand your underlying reluctance. Do not read the next section until you complete this activity. This activity will reveal much about you if you complete it without reading ahead. (If you are already sold on the idea of writing a business plan, you may skip the questions, go on to the next section, and begin to write your business plan.)

1. How do you feel about investing time in writing a business plan? How urgent do you think writing the business plan is compared to the other things you need to do as you set up your consulting business?

2. How do you feel about sharing your business plan with others? How about sharing it with friends?

3. How prepared are you to write a business plan? How knowledgeable are you about business plans in general?

4. How do you rate your writing skills? What concerns do you have related to your ability to write a business plan?

5. How thorough is your knowledge of consulting and your potential customers?

6. How confident are you that your plan will be accurate and that you will be 100 percent successful in the consulting field?

Evaluating Your Responses

Although the questions were related specifically to writing your business plan, your answers divulge much about you, such as how you approach tasks and where you may stumble as an entrepreneur. Here is how to evaluate your responses:

1. How did you respond about the time investment?   If you responded that you thought it would be a waste of time, perhaps you do not appreciate the value of planning and how much time you can actually save (or gain) by good planning. You may have responded that you think it's a good use of time, but you just don't have time now. The question is, if you don't have time now, when will you?

What might this answer say about you as an entrepreneur? Planning is critical to starting any business. Although some businesses fail due to a lack of financing or poor management, most actually fail due to inadequate planning. Don't fall into that trap. In addition, time will always be an issue for you. Once you begin consulting, you will find that you will often have more to do than time to do it. For example, you will find it almost impossible to find time to market when you're engrossed with a huge project. Yet you must market, even though you are too busy to market, or you may not have work when you've completed the project you are working on now. As a consultant, you will always be juggling many balls, and many of those balls will be urgent. You will need to find the time to do it all—and do it all with quality. You will find that there is always more to do than you think you will have time to complete.

Had I taken the time to develop a clear and complete business plan when I first started my company, I would have spent less time on hiring and developing staff and more time working with clients—what I actually loved doing.

Do you truly appreciate the value of planning? Are you always able to find time to complete critical events? How well do you juggle numerous tasks at one time?

2. How do you feel about sharing your business plan with others? One of the reasons for developing a business plan is to raise capital for your business, so, of course, you want to be comfortable discussing it with potential investors. But what about sharing it with family and friends? How appreciative will you be of their critiques? How objective can you be about suggestions that might change your plans? Some time ago, our company designed an off-the-shelf package for teaching process improvement skills. The kit, Process Tamer, is a proven process, was created using all the best adult learning theory, and was designed using only the highest-quality components. Because the price point was over $1,000, a publisher friend, Dick Roe, advised against moving forward. He suggested we were throwing away $100,000—the development cost. I didn't listen. He was right, and it was one of the costliest lessons of my consulting career. Are there other reasons you do not want to share your ideas? Are you worried about what others might say if you do not meet your goals? If you are reluctant to share your business plan because you do not want to hear the feedback, you may be missing valuable opportunities to hone your plan.

What might this say about you as an entrepreneur? Successful entrepreneurs must be receptive to others' comments. As a consultant, you must always be open to ideas and information. Remember that you are selling yourself. Therefore, you must make yourself more valuable. Feedback—whether supportive or critical—will make you more valuable. Even if you do not believe that the feedback is correct, the perception is there for a reason. Dig deeper, and learn more. Try to treat the information objectively. Of course, this isn't easy, but good consultants are thick-skinned. You must be prepared to receive feedback, hear bad consultant jokes, and even be called names, such as beltway bandit or con man. You must consider what you hear, and be objective about what you might do with the information. You'll be better for it.

Are you comfortable discussing your plans with others? How open are you to hearing negative feedback? How objective can you be to others' ideas? Are you able to discern valuable feedback from feedback that will not be helpful? Are you able to consider all ideas at their face value or for what might be behind them?

3. How did you respond about being prepared and knowledgeable about writing business plans?   Does your response indicate a reluctance to begin writing because you do not know how to write a business plan or because you do not have experience in developing one? If so, what have you done to address this gap? As a consultant, you will find yourself in many situations in which you will not know exactly what to do. Lucky (and rare) is the consultant who walks into every project knowing exactly what needs to be accomplished. If you do not feel confident about writing your business plan because you've never done one before, you are experiencing something that is consistent with consulting: starting something for which you do not know the answer.

What might this say about you as an entrepreneur? Entrepreneurs do not have all the answers to everything, but they do know how to find the answers. And when they don't know how to find the answer, they just begin. Consultants often need to be the epitome of Nike's "just do it." Consultants rarely have the luxury of giving up. Consultants are persistent.

This chapter will start you on your way to writing a business plan, but don't think that there is a right or a wrong way to write one. A business plan is simply your vision of what you want to do and the data that will support your ability to get from today to your future vision.

How do you respond when you hit a dead end? Are you willing to conduct research or use networking to resolve problems? Are you able to just begin and have faith that you will reach solutions?

4. How did you respond about your ability to write?   Writing is a basic form of communication with which all consultants must feel comfortable. I listed it in Chapter One as one of the skills required of a consultant. You will most likely need to write proposals, reports, letters, marketing materials, and many other documents. Your writing will project an image of you as a consultant. If you are not confident in your writing ability, you may wish to consider hiring someone to edit and proof your work. You may also want to register for a class at your local college or technical school.

What might this say about you as an entrepreneur? Recognizing a weakness and admitting to it are critical for success. The successful entrepreneur will find a way to overcome a weakness. As a consultant, you may not possess all the skills required for success. But if you have identified your weaknesses and determined how you will compensate, you are ahead of the game. You have at least two choices. First, you may learn the information or acquire the skills. Second, you may tap into someone else who has the knowledge or skill, for example, by hiring someone, working with a partner or adviser, identifying support contractors, or hiring your own coach.

What weaknesses or skill and knowledge gaps do you have as a consultant? What plans do you have to overcome them?

5. How knowledgeable are you about the profession of consulting and your customers? It's going to be difficult to write a business plan without this information. You may have a general idea of how you intend to consult, but specifics are necessary. If your response suggests that you still need to learn more, you may find that you will need to conduct more research, gather more data, and learn more before proceeding with your plans. Have you completed the step in Chapter One in which you interviewed a consultant? That is the very least that you should do. To gain more knowledge, you may want to join a professional organization such as the Association for Talent Development, the Association of Management Consulting Firms, the Institute of Management Consultants, or one that specializes in your unique area such as the Independent Computer Consultants Association or the American Society of Consulting Arborists. You may also want to interview potential clients whom you locate through your network.

What might this say about you as an entrepreneur? The most successful entrepreneurs have both depth and breadth of knowledge about their chosen field. As a consultant, you will want to commit yourself to learning everything you can about the profession and about your potential customers.

What do you still need to know about the profession of consulting? What organizations should you join? What books and journals should you read? How can you learn more about your customers?

6. How did you answer the confidence question? How confidently did you answer this question? If you have any self-doubts or fear of failure, a plan can do a great deal to eliminate those concerns. A well-done business plan will describe the concerns and provide the answers. Does your response suggest that you might fail at writing a business plan? In order to sleep at night, you need confidence that you can accomplish anything you set your mind to do.

What might this say about you as an entrepreneur? Entrepreneurs, especially consultants, must be passionate about what they do. Successful entrepreneurs are absolutely and unequivocally certain of success. I remember making the decision to move into the consulting field. As I played with the numbers—various formulas of how much work I expected, what kind of work I could do, and how much I thought clients might pay—I remember thinking, "I can't not succeed!" Passion about your success must start with you. If you don't believe in you, who will? Henry Ford said, "If you believe you can or cannot, you will prove yourself correct." You must believe that you hold the destiny of your business in your hands. You must feel confident of your success.

How confident are you that you will succeed as a consultant? Do you believe that you will achieve all your goals? Are you passionate about being a consultant? Do you believe in your own success? Will you be able to sell yourself with confidence?

The point of the preceding exercise was twofold: to identify what might be holding you back from writing a business plan and, more important, to find out what your excuses for not getting on with the business plan suggest about your consulting weaknesses. If any of the comments ring true for you, return to Chapter One to review your self-assessments. Pay particular attention to your responses to "Are You a Match for the Profession?" on page 9 and the "Entrepreneur Attitude Survey" on page 14. Now that you have a specific task to complete—writing your business plan—compare your responses in Chapter One against how you approached the task. Then develop your personal improvement plan here.

1. Would you change anything about your self-assessment? If yes, what?

2. What might you do to gain the experience, skills, knowledge, and aptitude for becoming a consultant?

3. How might you use other individuals to contribute or fill in what you might be missing?

When you are satisfied that you are ready to move on, begin to complete your business plan in the next section.

Write Your Plan

A business plan is generally five to 10 pages, plus several additional supporting documents. The plan may have several iterations and revisions. You may begin to write it and find that you need to conduct more research. You may also find that you haven't thought through all your ideas as thoroughly as you need and must revise your earlier business design. Don't get discouraged. It is far better to discover these things now than later.

The rest of this chapter is dedicated to helping you prepare a basic business plan. If you anticipate borrowing money to start your business, this plan provides the kind of detail required to attract investors. Use this book to jot down your ideas first. It will help you see where you will need to gather more information.

This book has not yet addressed every item that is in a good business plan. That means that you may not be able to answer all the questions presented, and that's okay, but you should make a concerted effort to answer most of them. Once you've captured your notes here, go to your computer and begin to write the narrative.

Your business plan has these sections: a cover page, table of contents, executive summary, business description, market analysis, competitive analysis, organization and management plan, marketing and sales plan, services or products, financial projections, and appendixes that contain financial documentation and supporting documents.

Quick • • • • • • • • ➤ TIP

Go to the Internet or call several publicly owned companies to obtain copies of their annual reports. Although you will not write anything nearly as elaborate as these publications, they will provide you with inspiration, examples of mission statements, and business language that is used.

Cover Page

The cover is the first page that your readers see, and it sets the tone for the rest of the business plan. First impressions are important, so present your best image. A cover page tells the reader that you take your business and this business plan seriously. The cover page provides all the information necessary for someone to get in touch with you. The cover also includes a date so that you know which edition of the plan you are using. When designing your cover page, consider adding some line graphics, a frame, a picture, or color. Add your logo if you have one.

Table of Contents

The table of contents provides another opportunity for you to impress your business plan reader by showing your organizational skills. The following example gives the suggested sections for a business plan.

Executive Summary

An executive summary is a brief overview of the entire plan. It will be easier if you write it last. The purpose is to tell the reader what to expect in the plan.

Business Description

This will most likely be the longest and the most important section of your business plan. Begin it with an introduction that states the purpose of the business plan. Follow this with a description of your consulting business. You may divide

Table of Contents

Executive Summary

Business Description
    Purpose
    Plans for the Business
    Business Activities
    Demographics of the Business

Market Analysis
    Estimated Market Size
    Estimated Market Dollar Value

Competitive Analysis
    Geographic Competition
    Competition's Strengths and
      Weaknesses

Organization and Management Plan
    Key Players
    Resources Available

Marketing and Sales
    Market Niche
    Pricing Strategy
    Market Tactics
    Literature

Service or Products
    Description
    Benefits

Financial Projections

Appendices
    Financial Documentation
    (list each)
    Supporting Documents
    (list each)

the description into your plans for the business, the work you will conduct, and the business's demographics. Use these questions to guide you:

- Introduction
  - What is the purpose of the business plan?
- Your plans for the business
  - What are the mission, vision, and/or purpose of your consulting business?
  - What are your goals for the business? (Your goals should be specific, measurable, and time bound.)
- The business activities
  - What specific activities does the business conduct to raise revenue?
  - What services or products will it provide?
  - Why do you believe your business will succeed?
  - What relevant experience do you bring to the business of consulting?
- Demographics
  - What is the name of the business? The address? Telephone and fax numbers? What is the email address? What is the URL for the website?
  - Who is (are) the owner(s)?
  - What's the business structure? If it is incorporated, where?
  - What information is important about the start of this business? For example, is it a new business or an expansion of an existing business? What is the start-up date?

Market Analysis

The market analysis will be most beneficial for financial support if you can quote statistics about consulting, your consulting specialty, or the industry you have chosen. You may find some of these data in industry journals or on the Internet. If you are consulting in the training area, *Training* magazine and the Association for Talent Development conduct research each year that might provide data for some consultants. The Big Four management consulting firms and *Consulting* magazine are other good sources.

Address these questions in the analysis:

- What industry or industries are you targeting?
- Are you in a stable, growing, or declining industry?
- What is occurring now or is expected to occur in the future that will affect your business either negatively or positively?
- Who are your current customers?
- Who are your potential customers?
- What are the demographics of your current and potential client base?
- What is the size of your potential market? What percentage of the market do you expect to penetrate?
- What's the estimated total market in dollar value?

Quick · · · · · · · · · ▶ TIP

Each of the Big Four management consulting firms (E&Y, Deloitte, KPMG, and PricewaterhouseCoopers) conduct research that may help you understand the consulting business. You could check their websites. *Consulting* magazine is another source of data and can be found at www. consultingmag.com.

Competitive Analysis

This section examines the competition you expect to face. It should answer these questions:

- Who is your competition?
- How would you describe your competition in the geographical and specialty areas you have targeted?

- How do your consulting products or services differ from those of your competitors?

- How do your competitors' pricing structures compare to yours?

- What experience do your competitors have?

- How strong is the name recognition of each of your competitors?

- What share of the market do these targeted competitors have?

- Is your competitors' business increasing, decreasing, or remaining steady?

- Why would someone buy from a competitor instead of you?

- How do your competitors market themselves?

- What are your comparative strengths and weaknesses in sales or marketing?

- What differentiates you from your competitors?

Organization and Management Plan

Answer these questions about how you intend to manage your consulting business:

- Who are the key players in your business? What are their duties, compensation, and benefits?

- If you are the sole employee, how will you manage all that needs to be completed? What is your starting salary?

- What resources are available if you need assistance?

- When do you expect to hire additional personnel—if ever?

- What experience do you bring to the business in marketing, sales, managing a business, and other supporting roles?

- What is your education level?

- What professional support will you use, such as an attorney, accountant, or banker?

- What banking services will you use, and where? What process will you use to establish credit?

Develop your Top 10 list of reasons that clients would hire you. This list will help you bridge the step from competitive analysis and management to your marketing plan. Yes, 10 is a stretch, but consulting is all about stretching!

Marketing and Sales

You can use the following questions to develop a simple marketing plan:

- Describe your market niche:
  - What size company will you serve?
  - What specific geographical area will you serve?
  - What kinds of organizations will you serve?
  - Will you serve special situations, such as start-ups or mergers?
- What are your pricing strategy and structure? How do they differ from those of your competitors?
- What marketing tactics will you pursue? What advertising? What promotion?
- How will you implement tactics throughout the year?
- What expertise will you use to develop your marketing plan?

  You will develop a more in-depth marketing plan in Chapter Nine.

Service or Products

You can use the following questions to define your services and, if you will have products, what kind:

- What will organizations hire you to do?
- Will you focus on general service topics or specific ones?

- Will you have products, such as surveys, instruments, software, or other tangible items you can sell?

  - How will they be developed?

  - When will they be ready for sale?

  - How are they connected to your services?

  - How will you cross-sell them?

Be sure to note how your services and products will benefit your clients and customers.

Financial Projections

Use these questions to write the narrative, and support your narrative with financial statements in the appendix:

- What assumptions are you making as a basis of the plan, such as market health, start-up date, gross profit margin, required overhead, payroll, and other expenses?

- What expenditures will you require for start-up?

- What are your cash-flow projections for each month of your first year?

- What are your three-year cash-flow projections?

- Where do you expect to find financing and under what terms? How will the money be used—for example, for overhead, supplies, marketing?

- Do you have a line of credit? How much is it?

- What is your personal net worth as displayed in a financial statement?

Appendices

The appendices contain documents that support your narrative. They may be divided into two sections or more. You may wish to include those listed here.

Financial Documentation

- Start-up expenses

- Budget

- First-year cash-flow projections

- Three-year projections

- Personal financial statement

- If you are already operating, an income statement from the past year

Supporting Documents

- Testimonials from satisfied clients

- References

- Demographic information

- Your resume, biographical sketches of your accountant, attorney, and others

- Industry data or demographics

Printing Your Business Plan

Once you've completed your plan, have it edited and proofread. You may wish to give it to several people—some who know the consulting business well, others who can edit for typos, spelling, and grammatical errors. Make the corrections, and print out a clean copy of your business plan on high-quality paper. You may wish to put it in a clear-front document binder. Combine it with your brochure and a business card for a complete product.

Plan to Use Your Business Plan

Whatever you do with the plan, do not put it on a shelf. It should become a working document that you refer to regularly. Your business plan contains important facets of your business. Keep the plan handy and use it when you need to make decisions. Check your business progress against the plan at least quarterly to keep yourself focused. And if something is not working, change your direction. Change your strategies if something isn't working. Keep your long-term vision in mind, and continue to move in that direction.

The process of creating your business plan prepares you to manage your business better. The planning actions force you to consider more aspects of your business, such as potential trouble areas, possible opportunities, or competitors you want to observe. That gives you lots of insight, but you can double the value by continuing to use your business plan. You might use it in several ways:

- Share it with suppliers with whom you may want to build a long-term relationship.

- Explain your business to potential clients.

- Use it to monitor your business performance.

- Use it as a tool to project problems early.

- Compare your projections with what is actually happening to determine your accuracy for envisioning the future.

- Share your plan with a potential new partner.

- Use it to ferret out your own strengths and weaknesses and then use that information to improve your business.

- Although you do not plan to fail, tracking your assumptions against actual numbers may provide an early warning sign and suggest a different path to avert failure.

- If you are ahead of projections, use the plan to determine the cause and if you can double or even triple your success.

- Use it as a planning tool if something unusual (good or bad) happens in the economy or the industry in which you are working.

- And of course, it is invaluable for convincing others to invest in your company.

Eventually your plan will need to be updated. Here are sources of data and information you might be able to use:

- Check in with your clients.

- Read the *Wall Street Journal.*

- Read journals from the industries in which you work. Subscribe to the *Harvard Business Review, Fortune* magazine, and *Fast Company* magazine to stay on top of business and management trends.

- Read books written by leaders you respect to inspire ideas for your consulting business.

- Attend industry conferences. Network with other consultants.

- Discuss things in your plan that aren't working with your mentor.

Use all the information from these suggestions to update your business plan and ensure that you are focused on your expanded vision.

Quick Start ACTION

Plan a Review

After you complete your business plan and before you leave this chapter, schedule a date with yourself (write it in your calendar or enter it into your electronic planner) to review your business plan. Schedule that date for six to 12 weeks out, depending on where you are in the process of establishing your consulting business. If you're just starting, do this in six weeks; if you have been consulting for some time, you could wait as long as 12 weeks. You decide what seems appropriate to you.

Alternatively, you may wish to consider bringing together a small group of advisers to provide an analysis of your progress. Perhaps start with your accountant (or maybe your banker and attorney depending on your relationship with them) and several colleagues whose opinions you value. Three or four people will be enough. They can serve as a quasi-board of directors for you. Send them your business plan now, and ask for their thoughts. In addition, ask them whether they would be willing to meet with you in four to six months for a review of your progress. The results will be well worth your effort.

Quick Start **LISTS**

Actions I Will Take

Ideas I Have

Questions I Need to Answer

Make the Switch Painlessly

6

In this chapter you will

- Identify opportunities to gain consulting experience before leaving your job
- Determine your transition plan

Gain Consulting Experience Before Leaving Your Job

You can gain consulting experience before you leave the safety net of your full-time job. You should identify several opportunities to get experience prior to leaving your job. For example, perhaps you can:

- Facilitate a weekend retreat for a local volunteer group.

- Conduct a team-building session for a civic organization.

- Offer your services on a freelance basis to a subsidiary or another firm in your company's business group.

- Design new software for a local school system.

- Teach a class at your community college.

Let me clarify one important point. This is *not* about working on your business on your employer's time. *Not at all.* You owe your employer a full day's work for a full day's pay. You can get experience before you leave your job by working outside of work hours. You can also volunteer for projects and tasks on the job that will give you the experience you need while at the same time assisting your employer.

If I sound a bit testy it's because I've just read a half-dozen blogs where the authors encourage readers to "take advantage of" their current jobs. Among other things, they suggest using your employers' data sources, replicating contact lists, printing materials, registering for training, contacting potential clients, and other actions for the sheer purpose of preparing to start a consulting business. This is *not* what I mean. But you can gain experience while benefiting your employer. How can you gain experience that you need before you leave your job?

Practice Being an Entrepreneur

Finding ways to practice your consulting is a good start. Everyone practices. Can you imagine an athlete who just shows up for a game without practicing or an actress who appears on stage opening night without practicing? Of course you can't.

Practicing your consulting skills is important, but even more important is practicing for the transition from employee to entrepreneur. What can prepare you for the move from employee to entrepreneur?

Build your skills and your network. You can benefit your company while gaining new skill sets you'll use as an entrepreneur. For example, ask for increased responsibility where you have an opportunity to practice building a budget, leading a team, selling a concept, marketing a new idea, communicating with other departments, or a multitude of other skills entrepreneurs use every day. You can begin to build a network of people who can advise you, recommend you, coach you, and provide feedback. Look beyond the workplace for your network. Who can you meet in the community, at conferences, and at local business meet-up events? Look for experts in various professional roles who could be potential colleagues or clients.

Begin planning on paper. Whether it is listing marketing ideas, designing your logo, or creating a start-up budget, you will be able to feed your thoughts into your business when the time is right. Determine the problem you can solve. I started my consulting business when most companies were using off-the-shelf training materials. The problem was that employees had difficulty translating examples from one industry to theirs. My solution was to design customized training programs for clients. What problem can you solve? How will you package your solution? These are all worthy of your planning—and yes, creating a business plan.

Shift your mindset from employee to business owner. Running your own business, being totally responsible for your income can be scary. What can you practice that will help make that shift? Try these mind hacks on for size. Risks are required for success. Failure is only a learning experience. Being uncomfortable is good for personal and business development. It's not selling—it's helping. Fear is only energy that fuels my business. I am my own boss. Each of these is a mind shift you'll make as an entrepreneur.

Building your skills and network; planning on paper; and shifting your mindset are all ways you can practice being an entrepreneur.

Getting Started

This book has focused on starting your own consulting business. There are several easy ways to enter the field:

As an employee. Many employment opportunities exist for you, from the small consulting firms in your city that have more work than they can handle to one of the large national consulting firms. A local company can provide you with a vast variety of projects, and you are likely to find yourself in charge of a project relatively quickly. A national company ensures name recognition if you later decide to start your own consulting practice. A national company also offers a salary about twice what you would receive if you worked for a smaller local consulting firm. You will probably have twice as much pressure and a large amount of travel as well.

As a subcontractor. Rather than become an employee, you could subcontract with one or several firms. You would have a less secure position than you would as an employee, but you would also have more flexibility, gain rich experience, and develop a sense of the market. It is likely that you would have time to begin a few of your own projects too.

As a part-timer. If you're not ready to take the plunge, you could consult part-time and keep your existing job. You could use your vacation time and weekends to conduct small projects. Be certain to keep your employer informed of any part-time consulting work. This arrangement is perfect for university professors or individuals who have vacation time or free time on weekends for additional work.

As a partner. You could buy into a partnership with one or more other consultants. You would be able to share the burden of expenses, marketing, and workload. The greatest drawback to this arrangement is the potential for conflict over business and personal preferences. These conflicts can vary from an unbalanced workload, to communication, to how much to charge. In the past couple of years, I have advised a number of virtual partnerships: the partners all have their own offices or locations, and many are located in different states. They come together periodically for synergy or to use specific expertise to collaborate on different projects. Partnership arrangements only work when a large amount of planning has occurred up front.

As a self-employed consultant. Starting your own consulting business is what this book is about. This is certainly the greatest risk among the choices, but it also presents the greatest potential reward and self-satisfaction.

How do you rate the five options? Perhaps if you have discovered that you do not have quite enough capital to start your own business now, one of the first four options might appeal to you temporarily. If you are not quite ready to leave your job altogether, you could try your hand at part-time consulting. Note here your specific considerations for a transition, as well as the most logical way for you to move into consulting

Discussions with Your Boss

Once you know you would like to move into consulting, make your boss your ally. Except in unusual situations where your boss is not approachable or your organization is not open to employees who want to strike out on their own, it will be helpful to you to meet with your boss to share your future plans. Use these suggestions to have a discussion that will boost your chances for a successful transition to consulting:

- No matter what stage you are in when you have your first discussion, be honest and candid about your plans. This common courtesy will most likely work in your favor.

- If you have developed your business plan, share it with your boss, and ask for input. Often, striking out on your own is a dream other people have but have not acted on for various reasons. I have found that they often enjoy living vicariously through those of us who have acted on our dreams. Your boss may be one of those people.

- Keep your boss informed about your progress; your boss can also be a sounding board for your ideas.

- Take care that you are not infringing on your employer's time as you plan for your future. That means you may wish to update your boss over lunch or after work hours as opposed to doing this during the workday. Remember to be a loyal, productive employee to the end.

- Do not bring up the fact that you might be able to consult with your current department or company. Although it is a great transition into consulting, it can appear to be a conflict of interest at this stage of your planning. It may appear to some that you and your boss are planning how to finance your business venture to the disadvantage of your current employer. Besides, sometimes the company will open that discussion and it becomes twice as valuable.

- Take care that you do not share your plans with too many people beyond your boss. Continue to maintain excellent working relations with your boss and others in your organization. You are probably excited about the prospects for your future as a consultant, but don't let your exuberance take over the office and your main purpose for being at this job.

- Guard against the short-timer attitude as you finish your duties or projects. Being professional straight through to the end gives you the best send-off as a professional consultant.

Determine Your Transition Plan

Making a transition from being a full-time employee to consulting will require some adjustment. A transition plan will help prepare you and those around you for a different lifestyle.

How Will You Transition to Your New Professional Life?

The ideal scenario is that your employer will offer you an opportunity to continue working on a project basis. The current shortage of employees has been a factor in creating that opportunity and is a win-win for you and your employer: you receive a guaranteed income to get started, and your employer receives your knowledge and experience while you both make the transition.

I was fortunate that my employer made this kind of offer to me. The department I was in was experiencing a huge turnover. When I applied for my boss's job and didn't get it because I lacked the credentials (I didn't have a degree at all and the job required a PhD), the company asked me to stay on for six months to train the new boss, three new trainers, and the new admin assistant. In exchange they would hire me as a consultant for several design projects. It was a perfect transition because it provided early income while giving me time to market to other potential clients.

What should you expect if you do this? Many make the transition with 60 percent of their salary or more and work less than 35 percent of the time. The rest of the time can be spent in setting up an office, marketing your services, and taking care of business issues.

Another option is working part time at both your job and at consulting. This is the least appealing of all the options, though, because you will constantly be pulled in different directions. You will be thinking about consulting when you should be working for your employer and concerned about your employer when you should be developing a marketing plan. And it undoubtedly will happen that the first consulting job you land will conflict with your company's annual meeting or some other important event that you must show up for.

What Transition Issues Are Ahead?

One transition issue to consider is how you feel about being a one-person company. For example, how will you respond the first time a client asks you about the size of your company? How will you feel about saying, "One. Me. That's it." Will you be proud of having gone out on your own? Or is there some stigma about being a consultant—and a lone one at that? How will you feel about doing your own typing, copying, errands, dusting, vacuuming, and trash removal? Another transition consideration is to have a plan ready to implement should you become ill. Could someone fill in for you? Under what circumstances?

A separate but related professional issue you may need to consider is working alone. Right now it probably sounds wonderful: you'll get to make all the decisions, do what you want when you want, and receive all the recognition. The drawback, of course, is that you would also assume all the risk, be responsible for all expenses, and have no one readily available with whom to discuss ideas and issues. A good idea is to set your support network up now. Whom will you call when you want ideas? Whom will you call when you want sound business advice? Whom will you call when you are overwhelmed? And whom will you call when you just want to go to lunch with someone who understands what you are feeling? Make a list now of your support network:

-
-
-
-
-
-
-

What Personal Transitions Will You and Your Family Make?

When everything goes smoothly, your family will readily accept your new role. Having a home office sounds great. Get up when you want, brew a pot of your favorite coffee, write a proposal in a sweatshirt and jeans, no traffic hassle. But how will your family deal with you underfoot all day long? How supportive will your family be when the big deal doesn't come through and you need to dig deeper into the family savings? How supportive will they be when you once again need to pass up a family outing because you must work on Saturday? How will they deal with getting business telephone calls at all hours of the night? You need your family's support—100 percent of it. You do not want them to say, "We told you so!" if something goes wrong.

Here are some transition considerations you all might need to discuss for a smooth change:

- How will you control household noise, such as your dog barking, during "business hours"?

- How will you have privacy when you are working?

- How will everyone share the house to meet everyone's needs? For example, what happens when eight five-year-olds are expected for a birthday party and you are in the middle of a long and important call?

- How will the family feel when you are late for dinner because your project is taking longer than you anticipated, yet you're only in the spare bedroom?

- How will Grandma feel sleeping on the couch because you have taken over the guest room as your office?

- How will your spouse react upon seeing the mess you made in the kitchen for a fast lunch—and didn't clean up?

- How will you deal with the ever-growing lawn outside your window when you have two proposals that are due this week?

- Will you be able to avoid the refrigerator as you walk past it for the twentieth time in one day?

In the space below, make a list of agreements you and your family will consider as part of your transition.

Where Will the Money Come From?

Even if you leave your job with the promise of six months of work, there is no guarantee that you will have your next projects lined up when that income stream ends.

You may become so tied up in the project your former employer has extended to you that you may not find the time to conduct the marketing that you should. Or your family may decide that you must take a vacation before you launch your new business. Or you may have been on the marketing warpath and have lots of possibilities, but nothing has materialized yet.

If you plunge right in to your new business without the benefit of support from your former employer, you will most likely need cash to start your business. Few people set aside enough money to start a business, no matter how far in advance they plan.

Where will the money come from? Consider these options:

- You could take money from your savings account.

- You could borrow against your retirement account (generally you can do this only if you'll continue working with your employer; also there will likely be steep penalties).

- You could obtain a loan on the equity in your house.

- You could borrow against your life insurance policy.

- If you have stocks, you could go on margin against them.

- You could obtain a line of credit from your bank.

- You could turn to the Internet and use a crowdfunded site such as Kickstarter, Indiegogo, or Crowdfunder.

- Your spouse could increase his or her contribution.

- You could sell something of value, such as a motor home or sailboat.

- You could cut back on some of your spending—for example, by not taking a vacation.

- You could obtain a business bank loan.

- You could apply for a loan from the Small Business Administration.

- You could ask a friend or colleague to sponsor you (remember that few things complicate a relationship like borrowing money does).

- You could borrow against your credit card (don't do this unless you have a great opportunity in hand and can pay it off quickly).

List all of your options and the amount that is available from each here:

Options Available   *How Much Money*

Based on your personal cash flow projections in Chapter Two and your business plan in Chapter Five, what shortfall do you expect over the next 12 months? What source will fund the shortage?

Month   *Shortage*   *Source of Funds*

Will you have enough money to easily get through the year? Have you planned for a worst-case scenario? You should be optimistic because positive thinking can take you a long way, but remember that it can't pay the grocery bill. You will be successful, but it may take longer than you anticipated.

Personal Financial Statement

If you think you may require a loan or expect to apply for a line of credit, you will need to provide a financial statement that summarizes your net worth. Most banks expect you to update it annually. A sample Personal Financial Statement is provided. Your financial software will likely have a financial statement form to use. Tap into your accountant if you need additional assistance.

Examine the issues identified in this chapter. Are you ready to make the move? What do you need to put in place?

Personal Financial Statement

Assets

Cash	_____
Savings accounts	_____
Stocks, bonds, and other securities	_____
Accounts, notes	_____
Life insurance (cash value)	_____
Rebates, refunds	_____
Autos, other vehicles	_____
Real estate	_____
Vested pension plan or retirement accounts	_____
Other assets	_____
	_____

Total Assets _____

Liabilities

Accounts payable	_____
Real estate loans	_____
Other liabilities	_____

Total Liabilities _____

Total Assets Less Total Liabilities = Net Worth _____

Source: The New Consultant's Quick Start Guide: An Action Plan for Your First Year in Business. Copyright 2019 by Elaine Biech.

Plan with Your Family

Sit down with your spouse, significant other, or other family members and discuss the issues identified in this chapter. How supportive will everyone be of your endeavor? Ask everyone in the discussion to identify what excites them the most about your planned consulting role. Also ask them what concerns them the most. Capture these responses here. Then, as a family, decide how you can build on the positives and what you can do to address the concerns.

What excites you the most about my becoming a consultant?

What concerns you about my becoming a consultant?

How can we build on the positives?

What can we do to address your concerns?

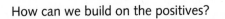

This chapter, although not dealing directly with developing your business, is one of the most important ones in this book. A successful transition plan is like a well-orchestrated football play. Planning ahead and thinking through all the possibilities are critical to a successful transition. Involve your family and others in the planning up front.

Quick Start **LISTS**

Actions I Will Take

Ideas I Have

Questions I Need to Answer

7

Setting Up Your Office—or Not

In this chapter you will

- Explore your options for an office location
- Prepare a plan to set up your office
- Learn how to manage your paperwork, including record keeping and invoicing
- Initiate your website

Office Location Options

You have many options when it comes to setting up your office. You could rent a standard office, lease space in an executive suite, or set up a home office. No matter where your office is, ensure that it projects the professional image you wish.

Renting Office Space

An office in a professional office building at a recognized location adds to your appearance as a professional. You may also feel more professional leaving your house every morning for the workplace. Leasing office space is often a long-term commitment (as long as three to five years), and if office space is in high demand, it could be costly as well.

Sharing Executive Suites

An office in an executive suite lies somewhere between a full-blown office and your spare bedroom. The popularity of these suites has grown due to the cost savings that are available by sharing a conference room, office support, telephone systems, and copy machines. Executive suites run the gamut for amenities, service, and quality, so shop around. Ask existing tenants about their satisfaction with services they receive.

Quick · · · · · · · · · · ▶ TIP

Want to ditch the office completely? Try an all-in-one service. Remote Year will take care of travel, lodging, workspaces, and other accommodations for consultants who bounce from city to city each month. Hacker Paradise and Unsettled offer variations of this service and are more about travel than working. If you do all your work remotely you could check them out too, although I think they may work better once you have completed your business start-up. The gig economy is fueling remote firms. You can learn more—and dream a bit—on their websites at www.remoteyear.com, www.hackerparadise.org, or www.beunsettled.co.

Using a Home Office

At one time, working out of your home was not cool. You would have been viewed as less than professional and not serious about your career. Today, all that has changed. Flexi-place, flex-time, and telecommuting arrangements are on the rise, and those who work at home are often envied by those who cannot.

Examine the advantages of having your office in your home:

- You work where you live.

- You have the flexibility of using time as you choose for both your business and your personal life, getting up at midnight to add an idea to your proposal, or being available to receive delivery of the new family television.

- You can deduct from your taxes a proportionate amount of your home's utility costs, taxes, mortgage, or rent.

- It's a low-cost option for start-ups that minimizes your risk.

- You don't have to commute.

There are also some disadvantages to having your office in your home:

- You work where you live.

- It may be inconvenient for meeting clients.

- There are many distractions, including chores, the refrigerator, television, and your hobbies.

- You may be lonely if you are accustomed to working in a large office with many people around.

- You may need to overcome the stigma of working out of your home if clients expect you to work out of an office.

- Creating dedicated space may be difficult.

Notice that "you work where you live" is both an advantage and a disadvantage. The choice really boils down to whether it is the right decision for you. As organizations recognize a need for their increased agility, they view home offices for both employees and consultants as a way to expand their options.

No Office at All

Most consultants provide their services at the client's place of business, so you do have the broadest of choices for office location. In fact, I spoke with one savvy young man who was certain that he did not need an office at all for the kind of consulting he did. He held up his laptop, tablet, and his smartphone and said, "With these I can do everything I need to for my clients at any location!"

Indeed, no office at all is certainly an option in today's world.

Weighing Your Options

You have other options in addition to the four listed. You could share office space with someone or sublease from others. In both of these cases, you will want to maintain your own separate identity for legal and professional reasons.

Answer these questions to help you decide the best option for you.

How much space do you need?

How much can you afford to pay for office space?

Is location important to your business?

What image must you project? To whom?

How long can you commit to stay?

How much time will you spend in your office?

Set Up Your Office

Once you've decided on space, you will need to ensure that you have furnished, equipped, wired, and supplied it with everything you will need.

An Office Is an Office, Not Your Family Room

This may seem like a strong statement, but if you have chosen the home office route, heed the warning. It may be cute when your four-year-old answers the telephone; it's not cute when the caller is the CEO you met at last week's conference. And the first time your dog barks as you are talking to a prospective client, you may understand why you must separate your office from the rest of the house. Create a plan for your professional telephone service as one of the first things you do. Do you need a fax machine? Only you will know that, but if you do, you may want two numbers: one for faxing and a second for voice calls. You can probably share your Internet service provider, but check into this to be sure.

Furnishing Your Office

Once you've settled on office space, you will need to furnish it with at least a desk, chairs, bookshelves, and a filing cabinet. While you're planning, think about where you will place the telephone, computer, printer, copy machine, and other equipment. Will you need extra tables on which to place some of these items? While you're at it, think ahead to a time when you may need administrative support. If you have several clients lined up, that time may come sooner than you imagine. Will that admin person meet with you in your office space? Complete work in the space? What are your options for the future?

Use the grid on the next page to lay out your office space. Each square counts as one square foot. Mark the location of the windows. Then measure your larger pieces of furniture and start sketching—with a pencil. Yes, of course there's an app for floor layouts, but you can probably have this completed before you locate an app and learn to use it! While you're doing this, also plan where you will need

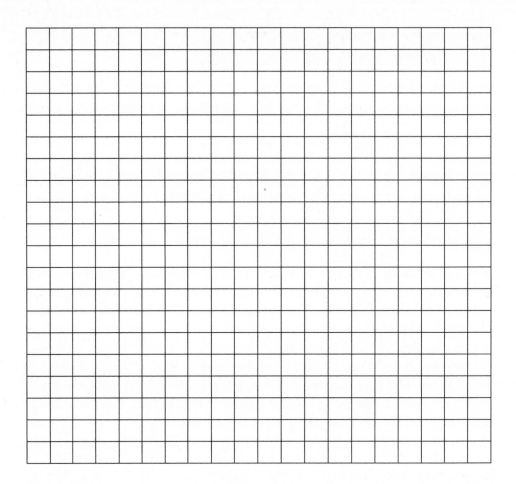

outlets and extra telephone jacks. And very important—lighting. Where's the natural light? Will you need additional lamps?

Planning Your Technical Needs

You will need a laptop, printer, and telephone system. With the right apps, you'll find a tablet comes in handy when meeting with clients. What about a copy machine? A lease can be reasonable, but if there is a copy shop or a printer near you, you may not be concerned about it immediately. Decide what you will need and try to condense to as few pieces of equipment as possible.

Get Wired. Accommodate all your electronic items with plenty of grounded outlets (if your home is not new, you may need to have some wiring completed). If you plan to have a landline, you may need to install telephone jacks (at least two separate lines: one for your fax machine and the other for a telephone).

Preserve Your Privacy. If you are a mobile-only phone user, you should not use your personal number for business. It may seem convenient and inexpensive, but the IRS frowns upon commingling business and personal use. In addition, you are exposing yourself to risk by allowing everyone to have 24-hour access to you. It will compromise your privacy, disrupt your work-life balance, and even increase your danger of exposure to hackers. How can you increase your control, flexibility, and security?

You have three options to preserve your privacy without compromising accessibility. First, you could purchase a second mobile phone with your business number. The advantage is complete separation. Second, you could expand the plan you currently have with your service provider. Third, you could obtain a virtual business phone number, which would be forwarded to your current phone, ensuring your privacy by setting the system to forward calls to your mobile phone during work hours or to voice mail when you are unavailable. Speak to your carrier about the options available to you.

Keep Clients Informed. Change your message regularly to let people know where you are. A generic message of, "I'm sorry I missed your call. Please leave a message and I'll get back to you as soon as I can," tells the caller nothing. Are you on another line? Are you off to the post office for 10 minutes? Are you on a two-week cruise? This is especially important when you will be out of reach for more than 24 hours. The best messages are up-to-date: "Hello, this is Carlos. Today is Tuesday, May 13, and I will be in meetings most of the day. I will pick up my messages at the end of the day and return your call no later than Wednesday morning. Thank you for calling!"

One dilemma for many consultants is that we are with clients during the day and unable to answer telephone calls, even if others call on our cell phones. This is why I generally provide my office number to clients. They can call and reach a live person who can either tell them what I am doing and how soon they can expect a response, and, in an emergency, my office staff can always reach me. If you will not have an office with support staff, update your messages regularly.

Supplying Your Office

When it comes time to purchase the office supplies you will need, there are two possible approaches. You can start by checking items on the following office shopping list and add other things to it. Or you can go to your local office supply store, grab a shopping cart, and walk up and down the aisles until you've found everything you think you will need. No matter which method you use, you will probably forget something. One last thing: Where are you going to store all these supplies?

Office Shopping List

- ☐ Paper
  - ☐ lined
  - ☐ notepads
  - ☐ printer
  - ☐ specialty or colors
  - ☐ other:
- ☐ Sticky note pads—size?
- ☐ Paper clips
- ☐ Binder clips
- ☐ Pens
- ☐ Markers
- ☐ Tape
  - ☐ strapping
  - ☐ cellophane
  - ☐ masking
- ☐ Stapler and staples
- ☐ Wastebaskets
- ☐ Extension cords
- ☐ Tape dispenser
- ☐ Surge protectors
- ☐ Stacking bins
- ☐ Bookends

- ☐ Banker boxes
- ☐ Pencil holder
- ☐ Flip chart pads
- ☐ File folders
- ☐ Pocket folders
- ☐ Envelopes
- ☐ Desk lamps
- ☐ Index cards
- ☐ Clock
- ☐ Dictionary
- ☐ Thesaurus
- ☐ Calendar
- ☐ Coffee cup
- ☐ Pencils
- ☐ Erasers
- ☐ Rubber cement
- ☐ Rubber bands
- ☐ Labels
- ☐ Stamp dispenser
- ☐ Scissors
- ☐ Letter opener
- ☐ Other things:

Stop at your post office to pick up these additional supplies:

- ☐ Stamps
- ☐ Priority mail folders
- ☐ Priority mail boxes
- ☐ Priority mail envelopes
- ☐ Express mail supplies

Paper, Paper Everywhere!

Consulting is not a paperless profession! You will use, throw away, send, sell, deliver, stamp, write on, print, read, and file more paper than you can imagine. Start a system early to keep yourself organized.

File, Don't Pile

Develop a filing system that works for you. File things with two important aspects in mind: ease of putting them away and ease of finding them! We use different colors of files to distinguish what's inside: blue for project files, yellow for office files, red for client resources and information, green for volunteer activities, tan for resources such as articles. You may start out with just one drawer and file everything alphabetically. Once you have been in business for several months, you will probably want to separate your drawers into categories, such as past client folders, originals, proposals, and resources.

A good filing system will keep you organized, prevent you from doing something twice, and save you time every day. The filing habits listed here pertain to paper files. Use the same advice for your electronic files. So, for example, purge your files regularly. And if you keep files that you are currently using on your desk, end the week by putting them in their proper spot. Go paperless when you can.

Good Filing Habits

- Grab a file as soon as you start a new project, client, or another category.

- Write the same thing first on each file tab; usually that means the organization or key word. If the file is about Mr. Hendrix from the San Francisco branch of Wells Fargo Bank, the file could be under H, S, or W. Decide what it's going to be now, and be sure to stick with it. It may not seem critical today, but in a year when you have 20 clients and 40 projects in 13 companies, you will be happy you have established a system.

- Put everything back in its place after you are finished with it, or …

- Store your filing in a small basket. Once the basket is filled or Friday rolls around—whichever comes first—file everything.

- Avoid duplicate files.

- Don't file anything that might not be helpful in the future.

- Condense your materials; that is, after a project, toss anything that will not be useful later.

- Purge your files regularly—at least once each year.

Establishing Your Record-Keeping System

Your records are the voice of your success. Good records can do two things for you:

1. They will tell you whether you are financially successful.

2. They will help keep you organized.

Quick · · · · · · · · · ▶ TIP

You might want to organize your desk drawer with monthly dividers. This method can help keep you organized and see at a glance what you have coming up in the months ahead.

After six months in business, your records should be speaking to you. They will tell you:

- Your total income and expenses

- Your profit or loss

- The number of customers you served

- The profit margins for each customer

- The accuracy of your projections

- How much money you will need for the next six months

- What you need to do to expand your business

Many of the forms you need were discussed in Chapters Three and Five. The forms that follow in this chapter are helpful to tell you how you're doing financially and to keep you organized.

Electronic Financial Records

Select your financial record-keeping system early. This chapter provides you with some basic forms; most accounting software will be able to generate the same forms and information easily for you. You might consider using QuickBooks Pro, Sage 50cloud Accounting, Freshbooks, FreeAgent, or Zoho Books.

Quick • • • • • • • • • • ▶ TIP

Consult your accountant when you select accounting software, so that your software will be compatible. Your accountant will also be able to assist you with setting it up so that it is useful to both of you and can be shared electronically.

Monthly Expense Worksheet/Record. This record is one that I examine regularly. I create a budget at the beginning of each year based on the past year and the projections for the upcoming year. You have already created a budget in Chapter Three. This form tells you whether you are taking in more or less income each month than you projected and whether your expenses are at the same level you projected. The implications are clear. See the form.

Monthly Expense Worksheet/Record

Account	Budget	Jan	Feb	Mar	April	May	June	July	Aug	Sept	Oct	Nov	Dec	Total
Accounting, banking, legal fees														
Advertising and marketing														
Automobile expenses														
Books and resources														
Clerical support														
Copying and printing														
Donations														
Dues and subscriptions														
Entertainment														
Equipment leases														
Insurance														
Interest and loans														
Licenses														
Meals														
Office supplies														
Postage														
Professional development														
Professional fees														
Rent														
Repairs and maintenance														
Retirement plan														
Salaries														
Seminar expenses														
Taxes														
Telephone														
Travel														
Utilities														
Total														

Source: The New Consultant's Quick Start Guide: An Action Plan for Your First Year in Business. Copyright 2019 by Elaine Biech.

Petty Cash Record. This is a simple way to track your petty cash at the end of each month. It will save you time when you try coming up with all those deductions for your accountant. Think it's a waste of time? Here's one example: If you pay $10 for parking when you visit your accountant once a month, that's $120 per year. By claiming it as a deduction you will save $40–50 in taxes. How many others are there? Meeting a client at Starbucks? Taking a potential client to dinner? Grabbing a roll of stamps at the post office? Paper towels at the grocery store? Buying candy for a training session? They all add up. See the sample Petty Cash Record.

Petty Cash Record					
			From: _____	To: _____	
Date	Where Bought	Item(s) Purchased	Expense Category	Initial	Amount
				Total	

Source: The New Consultant's Quick Start Guide: An Action Plan for Your First Year in Business. Copyright 2019 by Elaine Biech.

Revenue Projections. This form will track the dollar amount of the work you will do each month. It is critical for projecting cash flow. Use a form similar to the one provided here.

Revenue Projections

Organization and Project	Jan	Feb	Mar	April	May	June	July	Aug	Sept	Oct	Nov	Dec	Total
Total Revenue													

Source: The New Consultant's Quick Start Guide: An Action Plan for Your First Year in Business. Copyright 2019 by Elaine Biech.

Invoicing. If you want clients to pay you, you need to bill them. The next two forms provided here establish your invoicing process. The first is a sample of what is on an invoice (the bill you send to your client). The second (Invoice Summary) is a form to track whether clients paid you and when.

Invoice

INVOICE

100-000111-20XX

TO:	Ms. Cooper Garrison Cyber Systems, Inc. 513 Main Anywhere, VA 10000

Invoice Date: February 20, 20XX

For: Designed and conducted strategic planning
    for senior leaders
November 6–February 18, 20XX
Alexis Zick
    Consulting Fee $23,000.00

EXPENSES: Mileage Round Trip to Airport:
    80 miles @$.50 per mile .... $ 40.00
Airfare $810.00
Airport parking .... $ 30.00
Lodging $690.00
    Expense Total .... $ 1,570.00

Amount Due: $4,570.00

Terms: Due upon receipt

Payable to: ebb associates
Box 8249
Norfolk, VA 23503

Federal ID# 33-5333XXX

2 percent late fee charged per month for accounts due over 15 days

Source: The New Consultant's Quick Start Guide: An Action Plan for Your First Year in Business. Copyright 2019 by Elaine Biech.

Invoice Summary

Work Date	Organization	Trainer	Invoice Number	Date Billed	Date Paid	Facilitator Fee	Materials Fee	Expenses	Total Fee
Total									

Measuring Profitability. The Project Profitability form will help you measure your profitability. It tracks how much time you spent on the development or design, or both, and delivery of each project.

	Project Profitability			
Project Title	**Company Name**	**Development Time**	**Development Cost**	**Income**

Source: The New Consultant's Quick Start Guide: An Action Plan for Your First Year in Business. Copyright 2019 by Elaine Biech.

Staying Organized

Technology allows us the flexibility to stay organized. Yet, working alone and out of a home office presents problems for staying organized.

Take Care of You

- Plan your day around regular office hours and set a schedule. Most consultants work too much rather than not enough.

- Avoid distractions—especially all the things you know need to be done around the house.

- Learn to say no in various ways that are acceptable to you, such as, "That's thoughtful of you, but I need to pass."

- Focus on results, not how much time you invest.

- Get up from your desk regularly; walk outside; stay hydrated.

Use Your Time Wisely

- Maintain all contact information in one place—probably your smartphone, but don't delay adding new information.

- Group your incoming emails and schedule a time to address them—perhaps only twice a day.

- Schedule and stick to a specific amount of time to open social media.

- Keep your desk organized to save time and help you maintain focus.

- Unsubscribe to email newsletters and others you don't need.

Take Care of Your Clients

- Learn about your potential clients before officially meeting them—do your homework.

- Proofread all client documents—twice.

- Be prepared. If you think you should do it, do it.

- Attend to all details.

- Ask good questions.

What About a Website?

Setting up your office means setting up your website, too. Websites are as common as a telephone number these days. And you can locate people everywhere who are willing to help you design your site. When marketing, you will often be asked, "Do you have a website?" Having a website provides people with an easy way to get information about you and your consulting business.

To be sure your website projects your preferred image, hire a highly qualified web designer to assist you. Review other sites the individual has designed, and be sure the designer is a good communicator. Sometimes you will not know exactly what you want until you see a proposal. A good designer—that is, one who listens well—will be able to interpret what you want into a site that represents you and your consulting business accurately.

Ask for references, and establish a range of the design cost as well as what features that design will encompass. The initial design may be between $2,000 and $10,000, depending on how many bells and whistles you want to include.

Your website should be effective but simple. Don't allow the designer to make it so complex that it loses readers' attention. Be sure it is easy to maneuver and to locate information that is important to clients and potential clients. There is always an urge to do something creative and different, and I applaud you for that. But take care that your website is not so different from others that your clients have difficulty finding the information that they need. You don't want one of their first experiences with you to be frustrating!

Quick · · · · · · · · ► TIP

If you want to design your own website—which is perfectly doable—but want help from an expert marketing group, I have found none better than StoryBrand in Nashville, Tennessee. Check them out at www.storybrand.com.

You may choose to develop a site that allows interaction by including a quiz, a self-assessment, or a puzzle. Customize the site to meet the needs of clients who might visit. Ask yourself, "What would potential clients be likely to want to find on my website?" Begin with a page that defines the problem you will help them solve. The site should be about them—not just you. Of course, you'll include information that defines your company and the kind of work you do. You may wish to add a client list, testimonials, or a list of services and products you provide. Ensure that potential clients can email you while visiting your site and ask your designer how you could capture names of interested visitors for follow-up.

Many people forget that individuals sometimes go to a website to find other ways to contact people or to determine where a business is located. Therefore, don't forget to include a telephone number, the address where your business is located, and its mailing address if it is different from the street address.

Select an URL for the website that is easy to remember and makes sense to potential clients. Using your corporate name is usually the best.

Once you have a website, print the address on your business cards, stationery, pamphlets, and anywhere else it will be useful. Remember that the Internet is not intended to broadcast your message like other marketing media. Instead, you need to publish your website address so clients can find you and your information.

Finally, maintain your website regularly. Visit it often and respond to emails and other requests within 24 hours. If you have a calendar posted, keep it up-to-date and refresh your website every month or two.

Quick • • • • • • • • • ▶ TIP

Launching your website is a perfect excuse to contact potential clients and market to them. Once your site is up and all the bugs are worked out, contact your clients and potential clients to obtain feedback about the site.

The App Age

There is an app for everything. We asked our colleagues to list those they found the most beneficial to them. I encourage you to choose several, check them out, and determine which would make the most sense as you set up your consulting business.

Getting Organized

- EVERNOTE syncs notes across mobile and desktop devices.

- TRELLO is a project management app that tracks workflow and assignments.

- DROPBOX is a platform for storing and sharing files on the cloud.

- MAILCHIMP helps you manage your mailing lists and can be used to easily create and send newsletters.

- EXPENSIFY provides a way to track your business trip expenses.

- SCHEDULEONCE is a service that allows you to send someone a link to your schedule to more efficiently schedule a call or meeting.

- TIMELY is a time-tracking app that integrates your calendar, GPS, selected files on your computer, and more.

- FANTASTICAL is a calendar app to send reminders of events.

Communicating

- SLACK is an instant messaging platform to easily send and organize a team's communication.

- SKYPE is a video conferencing app used by the masses.

- ZOOM can be used for one-on-one calls, meetings, and for webinars.

- TUNNELBEAR will help you protect against hackers.

- Google HANGOUTS is a chat, call, and messaging tool.

Other Tools

- THINKIFIC is an intuitive interface to create an online course.

- TEACHABLE is a platform to create and sell online courses.

- WEEBLY is an easy drag-and-drop site to build your website.

- WORDPRESS can help you create a website or blog.

- PROPOSIFY helps you create a professional-looking proposal.

- GRAMMARLY helps consultants check their grammar on reports or proposals before sending them to clients.

- SURVEYMONKEY is a free tool for creating surveys.

- POLLEVERYWHERE is useful for interactive surveys.

- YOURTRAININGCONSULTINGBIZ.COM is an online course that will walk you through step-by-step startup of your consulting business.

There are so many. Which of your favorites did I miss? Which of these apps do you think will make your life as a consultant easier? Start a conversation with other consultants you know to help you decide which will be the most useful to you.

· ·

You've identified an office location, prepared a plan to set up your office, established your record-keeping system, and reviewed what you need for your website. Now all you need are clients. Chapter Eight will guide you through that challenge.

Quick Start **LISTS**

Actions I Will Take

Ideas I Have

Questions I Need to Answer

The New Consultant's Quick Start Guide

Finding Clients

8

In this chapter you will

- Determine your niche in the market
- Analyze your competition
- Identify your first clients
- Create a plan to land your first work

Determine Your Market Niche

In Chapter One you declared that you were a _____ consultant who helps your clients to _____, which benefits them _____. We'll begin with this statement as you identify your market niche.

Your *niche* is the position you wish to occupy that sets you apart from as many other consultants as possible. This niche may be based on the type of service or product you provide that solves a client problem, the type of client or industry you serve, how you provide your services, or the specific expertise or experience you have that validates your services.

So far you have explored your areas of expertise, the experience you've had, your natural abilities, the benefits you could provide a client, the results that might be valuable to a client, and other things. To identify your niche in the marketplace, you will examine what you will do from a client's perspective and begin to describe your clients more specifically, thus homing in on your potential client base.

To what part of the market will you offer your consulting? You need to clarify this before you create your marketing plan in the next chapter. A portion of your marketing plan will target a market segment on which you will focus your marketing efforts. You need this focus so that you are not trying to be everything to everyone.

The opportunities available to you as a consultant are broad. You must begin to identify your niche—what you profess to do. This is a long-time consulting dilemma: if what you claim you can do is too broad, your expertise may appear shallow; if what you state you do is too narrow, it decreases your chances for locating work. To say it another way, the more generalized you are, the less credible you'll be in potential clients' eyes; the more specialized you are, the more difficult it is to find and acquire the narrowly defined business.

Even understanding this, you must still determine what sets you apart from other consultants. What is unique about what you offer? A new consulting company can be successful more easily if it focuses on a specifically defined market. If you are a small company, you will be more successful creating your own niche than trying to compete against larger, more established companies that may be your competitors.

In Chapter Six I mentioned that when ebb associates started, we decided to offer customized training programs to clients. At the time, we didn't really understand that we were selecting a unique niche. What we did know was that most participants in the training sessions we offered complained about not being able to transfer what they learned in a training session to their workplaces. It was a problem that needed a solution. We were able to do what the large training vendors could not: we could focus on one client at a time and design exactly what that client required. Now that desktop publishing is widespread, that service is not so unique. However, at the time, we made our mark in the training consulting field by filling a unique need and along the way identified our niche in the marketplace. We were fortunate that the skills and attitude required for that niche are some of the same required to conduct consulting of any kind. We easily moved into other areas, such as strategic planning and team building.

How can you discover and describe your niche? First, review the previous chapters, where you focused on what you could offer. Second, determine if potential clients have a need that is not being fulfilled or a gap that is not closed completely by your competitors. You might think of it as a problem that needs to be solved. Third, identify the services and products that you could deliver to meet the need, close the gap, or solve the problem.

This chapter leads you through several exercises to help you uncover your niche. The exercises will help you to explore your expertise and potential client base, present a process to discover what clients need, and suggest how you can scrutinize and compare your competitors.

Begin by using the newspaper industry's method of uncovering the facts—answering the who, what, where, when, and why questions. Answer the questions under each heading that follows to identify your marketing niche and describe your client. Where appropriate, answer these questions from your potential clients' perspective.

Who?

Use these questions to begin to develop a profile of your potential client:

- Will you target for-profit or nonprofit organizations?
- If you target for-profit, what sector will be your focus—for example, manufacturing, service, retail?
- What specific industry will you target—for example, healthcare, hospitality, food service, construction, high tech?
- If you target nonprofit, what sector will be your focus—for example, associations, educational institutions, or local, state, or federal government?
- What size organizations will you target—for example, Fortune 500, medium, small? You may choose to identify the size by number of employees, revenues, or something that is unique to the industry; hospitals, for example, measure size by the number of beds.
- What level in the organization will you target—for example, front-line employees, first-level supervisors, managers, or executives?
- What's the structure of the group you will target—for example, new teams, intact work groups, individuals?

What?

Use these questions to pull together the expertise and experience that you explored in Chapter One. Now is the time to identify the specifics:

- What will your customers want from you? How will this differ from what they expect from other consultants?

- Will your clients have a special situation—for example, start-up, family-owned, merged, or high-growth businesses?

- What role will your customers see you conducting—for example, trainer, facilitator, coach, technical adviser, process consultant, content expert, support, resource, strategic planner?

- What topic of expertise will your client expect—for example, team building, computer programming, leadership, time management, investing, regulatory laws, marine biology, accounting, cybersecurity, construction, inventory control?

- What's special that sets you apart from other consultants?

Where?

Part of your work in Chapter Two was to identify where you would ideally like to work. It is probable that clients in your chosen industry may be found everywhere. Therefore, location may have as much to do with your preference as anything else:

- Based on the lifestyle you have described in Chapter Two, where will you be working?

- Will your focus be local, statewide, regional, national, or international?

- Do your selected industries suggest a specific locale, such as furniture manufacturing in North Carolina, high tech in Silicon Valley, importers in San Francisco, New York, and other coastal cities?

- In what surroundings will you work—for example, rural, village, city? What size city (if a city is your choice)?

- Will you narrow your market niche by climate?

When?

These questions will help clarify the time-bound aspects in your consulting niche:

- Will you focus on long-term or shorter contracts?

- What's the range in length of the contracts you will target?

- Will the time range be different for different services?

- Will you provide follow-up services?

- How much repeat business will you target?

- At what point in the problem-solving cycle would you enter—for example, identifying a problem, identifying the cause of the problem, identifying the solution, or implementing the solution?

Why?

In Chapter Three, you identified the value you add for which a client would be willing to pay. Use that information to help you focus your marketing niche based on why a client would hire you:

- Why would a client view your experience and expertise worthy of hire?

- Why would a client hire you over your competition?

- Why might a client see you as adding flexibility to the organization?

- Why would a client look to you to offer a fresh, objective point of view?

- How efficient do you believe you are?

- Would clients hire you if they needed to reassure regulatory, safety, or legal authorities about something?

Is There a Need?

Without getting into actual market research, it is important to identify whether there is a need for the niche you have just identified. You may have identified a service that enables you to use what you like and what you know, but will the client base you identified want to buy what you offer?

Quick Start **ACTION**

Is There a Client Base?

Before you move forward, be sure that there is a client base ready and waiting for your consulting service or product. Select three organizations that match the characteristics of the organizations you just described. Then follow these steps and record what you learn here.

1. Identify specific individuals in organizations to whom you will eventually sell your services. If you do not know anyone personally, you can introduce yourself to someone. Do this by checking the company's annual report (which you can usually obtain on request or by checking the company's website) or calling the receptionist and asking for the name of the person in the position to whom you wish to speak.

2. Call the individuals, and tell them that you have a business concept you would like to discuss and about which you would value their opinions. Ask if they have five minutes for you. If not, ask if there is a better time. If the person responds positively, move forward. If the person responds negatively, say thanks, and move to your next candidate.

3. Briefly explain your business, its purpose, and how it might benefit the individuals and their businesses by cutting costs or increasing profits.

4. Ask whether they think they would see a need for your services in the future. Probe to find out why they responded the way that they did.

5. Thank them for their time.

6. If they responded positively, ask them if you could send more information, a letter, or a brochure once your company is up and running. (This might be your first marketing action—and perhaps your first client. My first exploratory visit turned into my first paying client.)

7. Be sure to follow up with a handwritten thank you note on the same day you made the phone call.

8. Record your information:

Company Name/Individual	Position	Response

1.

2.

3.

Analyze Your Call

Did the phone calls encourage or discourage you? If you are positive about moving forward, spend some time analyzing your competition next. If the phone calls were not positive, you might analyze your calls. Did you call the right people? Did you call the right companies? Did you demonstrate the right attitude? Should you call others? Did you sell your concept well? Was the timing right? Did everything go as you planned it? What might you do differently with subsequent calls?

● ●

Who's Your Competition?

The only way to answer this question is to know your industry, know your competition, and know yourself.

Know Your Industry

Keep an eye on your competition. Being a consultant can be lonely, and this means you may find yourself outside the information loop—what's happening in the industry in which you work and in business in general. You may find being alone psychologically difficult; it can also be financially devastating if you do not stay on top of what's happening in your field. What's happening in the field and what your competition does will affect your marketing direction.

Be aware of trends. How will a surge in growth or mergers or buyouts affect your consulting services? How will the latest management fad affect the message you deliver to your clients? How will changes in technology affect your products and services?

How are your clients addressing these changes? You can observe this with what you already have available. Read your professional journals and key bloggers with these questions in mind: Who's advertising? What are they selling? What's their focus? Who's writing articles? What are the topics? Attend conferences with these questions in mind: Who's presenting? What are they espousing? What's the buzz in the hallways? Attend trade shows: Who has a booth? What are they selling? What message are they delivering? Visit bookstores: Who's writing? What topics are being published?

Take time now to page through your most recent professional journal. What did you learn about your competition from reading it? Scout out their websites. What is unique about their services? How do your services compare?

Know Your Competition

Review the information from your business plan in Chapter Five to get you started here. You need to understand your competition so that you can set yourself apart from it. Many savvy consultants will tell you not to worry about your competition, but to just do what you know is best. This may be good advice once you are established; however, as a start-up you need to know what's out there. You will want a clear sense of what differentiates you from your competition before you write your marketing plan in Chapter Nine.

Identify three competitors, and complete the Competitor Comparison chart so you can compare your business to the competition.

Competitor Comparison

	Your Practice	Competitor 1	Competitor 2	Competitor 3
Name				
Location				
Fees charged				
Years in business				
Specialty area				
Client type				
Client location				
Why clients use them				
Name recognition				
Image				
Quality				
Other				

Source: The New Consultant's Quick Start Guide: An Action Plan for Your First Year in Business. Copyright 2019 by Elaine Biech.

Quick · · · · · · · · · · ▶ TIP

Use your network. If you are unable to answer the questions in the Competitor Comparison chart about your industry, tap into your network. You might talk to friends in business, your potential clients, or another consultant who is outside your geographical or content area. Professional organizations also provide opportunities to talk with your competitors at conferences and chapter meetings. You should belong to at least two professional organizations that support what you do.

Know Yourself

Why will someone hire you? That's the bottom line of creating your niche. Consider some of these and check all those that apply. Will your clients experience:

☐ Faster time to market

☐ Decreased expenses

☐ Increased revenues

☐ Increased market share

☐ Improved customer retention

☐ Increased innovation

☐ Improved agility

☐ Improved efficiency

☐ Increased employee retention

☐ _____

Competitive Analysis

A competitive analysis compares your strengths and weaknesses to your competitors'. Use the information you uncovered to organize your thoughts and make the comparison:

Who are your strongest competitors?

In which geographical areas will you have the most competition? The least? What does this tell you about where to focus your energy to find new clients?

How do your competitors' specialty areas compare with yours? How will this affect your ability to generate business?

How will your competitors' pricing affect your ability to get business?

How will your competitors' experience, name recognition, image, and reputation for quality affect your ability to compete? How might you take advantage of this in finding new clients?

What are your competitors doing right? What could you do better?

What might you be able to offer that differentiates you from your competitors?

Quick ·········▶ TIP

Read your junk mail. Wallow in your junk mail! The direct mail you receive in your mailbox and your inbox every day is a marketing gift. You can use it to learn what your competition is doing, how to write more effective marketing letters/emails, how to design brochures, and what trends are hitting the profession. Don't bemoan the fact that your mailbox is stuffed with junk mail every day. Instead, be thankful for all the market research that has just been dumped in your lap!

Go one step further. Almost all your competitors will offer lead magnets to encourage you to give them your email address. Go on their websites and study their tactics, their tools, and their philosophy. Sign up for their free offers. Download their ebooks. What can you learn?

Your Niche

Examine everything you have identified about you, the clients you will target, and your competitors. How would you summarize the niche you have selected for yourself? What is special about your services that sets you apart from the rest? How are you defining your client base that sets you apart? Can you describe what you do that benefits your clients in one sentence?

Use these questions as a guide to write your niche statement here.

Identify Your First Clients

You have clarified your niche. Now it's time to specify the organizations in that niche by name. Who will be your first clients?

You are in control of identifying your first clients. Yes, you will acquire some work through referrals from friends, family, and colleagues. You may have some work from your current (or past) employer. And you may have some work come your way through people you meet at professional meetings or conferences. Some of this work may be related to your niche, but much of it may not. As you begin, however, you will most likely not turn any of it down.

Examine the niche statement you wrote at the end of the previous section. Now identify 20 organizations by name that meet your criteria and with which you would like to do business. This is not the time to be shy, timid, or modest. Go for it. Are you thinking that Microsoft is too large? Perhaps Harvard is too prestigious? Or General Motors is too impenetrable? Don't let size, prestige, or reputation scare you. The people who manage organizations need good consulting, no matter what the size of the company supplying it is. I've always said, "Go for the big fish; you'll spend the same time baiting the hook." You will invest the same amount of time marketing to large organizations as small, and the payoff may be much greater.

Larger organizations have larger consulting budgets, they generally have a greater need, they are more likely to hire consultants for repeat work, and they are often willing to take a risk with new consultants. So don't be intimidated by size. To whom do you want to provide your consulting services? Identify 20 organizations here that you would like to hire you as a consultant:

1.

2.

3.

4.

5.

6.

7.

8.

9.

10.

11.

12.

13.

14.

15.

16.

17.

18.

19.

20.

Land Your First Work

You've identified your 20 top candidates. Now how do you get to them? You could just make a phone call and talk to them. That's called *cold calling*, and usually isn't much fun. I have a friend in sales who lives by cold calls. He says he makes 100 phone calls to find 10 people who will talk to him. Of those 10, two will agree to meet with him in person, and one will purchase his product. That doesn't sound like fun to me.

Quick · · · · · · · · · ▶ TIP

You've probably heard about job boards, used by clients who post projects and consultants who bid on them. But before you jump to the idea that this is a great way to land your first work, know that consultants and freelancers of all types are frustrated with them. Complaints include low pay, poor quality, poor fit, and that they're difficult to use. The general consensus is that they have a lot of potential, but at this time they are a general waste of time. (If you are looking for a problem to solve, this might be it!)

Warm Up Your Cold Calls

There is a way to warm up those cold calls. And although the process takes some investment up front, the odds of an immediate sale are much greater, you will begin to build relationships for future sales, and it's much more fun.

Here's the process I use:

1. Identify 20 or 30 organizations you wish to target. Begin with that many because some will fall out along the way: you may have difficulty locating information about them, or you may change your mind about wanting to work with them based on information you learn.

2. Open one Company Profile form for each organization you have targeted in your computer. Complete whatever information you know about it.

Company Profile

Company Name _____

Address _____

_____

Website _____   Telephone _____

Employees _____

Management Positions

_____   _____

_____   _____

_____   _____

_____   _____

Products and Services _____

_____

History _____

_____

Future Plans _____

_____

Financial Information _____

_____

Organizational Philosophy _____

_____

_____

Relationship to My Consulting Services _____

_____

Additional Relevant Information _____

_____

Resources Used _____

Source: The New Consultant's Quick Start Guide: An Action Plan for Your First Year in Business.
Copyright 2019 by Elaine Biech.

3. Next, check out the organization's website. Capture all the information that might be pertinent to services you could offer the organization. You are trying to gather enough information for two reasons: first, to learn as much as you can about the organization, and second, to have enough information to compose a unique, personalized letter that will grab the reader's attention.

4. If the organization is publicly traded, you should be able to obtain the annual report.

5. Use the Company Profile form to organize the information you find.

6. You probably will not get all that you need from the website. Therefore, you will continue your research at other sites. First, conduct a general search on the Internet. This may uncover a wide variety of information—some useful, some not. Continue searching for what you need.

7. If you still need more information, you may be able to find information at your library—especially about local companies. You can check the local business magazines, journals and periodicals, local business newsletters, local newspaper, the city directory, manufacturer and business directories, and any other useful resources. Each of these has an index that makes it easy to research a list of clients in a couple of hours. If you can't find it on the Internet, your friendly local librarian is sure to assist.

8. Once you have gathered all your information, compose a letter to each of these clients. Follow these guidelines:

   - Be certain you are sending the letter to the right person.
   - Double-check the person's title and spelling of the name.
   - Focus on the recipient in the first paragraph, and show you know what's important to the organization. Never ever start the letter with "I."
   - In the next one or two paragraphs, connect the recipient to the need for consulting services and establish your qualifications. Determine how you can either save the company money or deliver a return on their investment. You must customize these paragraphs as well. For example, a list of your experiences should relate to the recipient's need or industry. If you can't do that yet due to a lack of experience, provide your most impressive information to date, but relate it to the potential client.

- In the final paragraph, tell the person what to expect. Maintain control of the process by saying, "I will call you within the week to schedule an appointment to . . . . You lose control when you say, "Give me a call to discuss . . . ."

9. Mail your letter, and follow up as promised.

I've used this process for over 20 years with remarkable success. I usually find enough information for about half the potential clients I target. Ninety-five percent of all recipients are interested enough to speak to me, and more than half of them agree to meet me within the month. Of those, who meet with me, half become clients within a year. The rest become contacts, resources, or clients in the future because I stay in touch with them.

You can have this same success rate. And you will find that this is a very positive way to begin a client-consultant relationship.

The Sample Letter is an example of the type that I use to contact potential clients.

Sample Letter

July 12, 20XX

Wayne B. Miller, President
Auto Glass Experts, Inc.
230 North Landing Road
Norfolk, VA 23513

Dear Mr. Miller:

Auto Glass Experts is one of Norfolk's success stories. In just over 20 years you have transformed an innovative idea into a successful business spanning five states. Your expertise for repairing windows in cars, trucks, and heavy equipment is now available in 23 locations, with sales pushing $60 million. Strong management and hard-working employees achieved these results.

At ebb associates we recognize the important role employees play in the successful growth of any company. Further, we have found that improving employees' communication skills results in improved productivity and increased profit. Do you realize that just one $500 listening mistake by each of Auto Glass Specialists' 400 employees can result in a loss of $200,000 each year? Improved communication skills can decrease mistakes, increase your profits, and improve customer relations.

ebb associates specializes in communication training. We present workshops and seminars focusing on improved communication and will custom-design a program to meet your needs at Auto Glass Experts. Our clients, including Tenneco Automotive, Chrysler, and Cardinal Glass, recognize our commitment to meeting their needs, providing excellent follow-up, and obtaining results. We'd like to help you, too, so that you can improve the quality and increase the quantity of work by maximizing the potential of your human resources.

I would like to call you within the week to schedule an appointment to discuss how we can assist you to meet your goals at Auto Glass Experts. I am enclosing a list of the course titles that we can customize to meet your specific needs. And we'd be happy to design a new class that meets your needs. I look forward to meeting and working with you.

Sincerely,

Elaine Biech
ebb associates

Source: E. Biech, *The New Business of Consulting* (Hoboken, NJ: John Wiley & Sons, 2019).

Reviewing Results

Examine the letter carefully. What do you notice about this letter? If you were Mr. Miller, what would encourage you to meet with me? How can you make this process work for you?

I work on a batch of letters all at once to save time. If I am going to focus on this task, I find that completing a group takes less time per letter. I will start with my original list, knowing that some prospects always drop out along the way because I can't find enough information or I learn something that makes them an unlikely candidate. In addition, I get myself into a sell zone and make all the phone calls within the same week and schedule sales calls soon after.

I am frequently asked if the letter can be emailed. The answer is, "Of course it can." I know for a fact that it will not be read as closely, if at all, as a letter that arrives in an envelope with a stamp. I am not a psychologist, so I don't know why. I have my guesses. The mechanism to deliver your message is up to you. Let me know how this process works for you.

What About the Referrals You've Received?

Do follow up with every referral you receive from friends, family, and colleagues. Even if the project is not quite right for you now, the meeting may lead to other work in the future. And you may also ask potential clients to refer you to someone who might be able to use your services. (This is networking at its finest.)

Select one referral right now, and make an appointment to explore possibilities. You will find this meeting helpful in several ways. First, you will get an idea of what to expect when you visit a potential client. Second, you will have an opportunity to practice selling your services. Third, you will learn what needs clarification as you describe what you do.

A Dozen Quick Prospecting Ideas

Prospecting for clients can be fun. It often puts you in touch with lots of people. Some of these prospecting ideas might resonate with you:

1. Call your college roommate and ask for a referral.

2. Write an article and email it or send it to potential clients.

3. Pass out two business cards to everyone you meet: one to keep and one to pass on.

4. Be a guest on a local talk show.

5. Find a great article in a recent business magazine. Purchase a dozen copies of the magazine, mark the article with a Post-it Note, add a personal note, and send it to a dozen clients you've contacted.

6. Call several members of your network and ask them to suggest others you might help.

7. Purchase the latest business book in multiple copies and send to several potential clients with a personal note from you.

8. Identify a great podcast series, such as Halelly Azulay's *TalentGrow Show*, that focuses on leadership. Send the link in an email to a dozen potential clients.

9. Submit a proposal to speak at a conference that you anticipate your clients will attend. Focus your submission on a problem clients would want you to solve.

10. When you are accepted to speak at a conference, gather business cards for a drawing at the end of your presentation. Prizes could be books that interest the audience. Follow up after the conference with information about you and your presentation and how it can solve your attendees' problems.

11. Attend a local networking event. They are often listed on Eventbrite.

12. Attend local chapter meetings; volunteer to be the membership chair or for another task that allows you to meet others.

If you already have a client or two, the best prospecting may occur inside that same organization. Plan to meet other department heads within the company. Other leads might occur if you ask the person you are working with to introduce you to others. You could provide a prewritten virtual introduction email for your colleague to use. When you follow up, ask for 15 to 20 minutes and then honor your time commitment. If the discussion is going well the potential client may ask you to stay longer. Even if there is no current requirement, if you created a positive atmosphere and connected, you will likely hear from the individual in the future.

You Have an Appointment—Now What?

Okay, you have an appointment with a client. What do you need to know before you go? Be sure you know at least the following: the purpose of the meeting, who will attend, how long the meeting will last, and exactly where it will be (office, conference room, and so forth). What do you do once you get in the door?

Your initial meeting is critical. It sets a tone for the rest of your relationship. You may come prepared with a PowerPoint presentation, materials in a bound folder, and a precisely worded presentation. That's not my style. My preference is to create a conversation with the client, learning as much about them as possible. Here's a guide that has been successful for me:

- Read the client. Take cues from what the client says and does to determine whether to make small talk or get right down to business.

- Listen more than you talk and listen for understanding. Read between the lines.

- Ask pertinent, thought-provoking questions. Prepare a list of five to 10 questions based on what you know about the situation. (Some samples are provided in the next section.)

- Address their future ideal. Identify how you can make more money for your client or help them cut costs. If you are meeting with a nonprofit, how can you help them achieve their mission faster, more efficiently, or with higher quality?

- Address all meeting attendees by name. Follow your client's lead about whether to use a title or first name or surname.

- Exude self-confidence without arrogance.

- Project a professional image with a firm handshake, appropriate attire, high-quality materials, and a genuine interest in the client.

What to Ask Potential Clients

General Questions

- What does your company [division, department] value most?

- What is your company's [division, department] number-one priority this year?

- What is your strategy to achieve that priority?

- What company's [division's, department's, leadership team's] strengths will help to achieve your priority?

- What challenges must you overcome to meet your priority [goals, objectives, mission]?

- What are the greatest challenges you will face over the next two years?

- What opportunities for improvement would alleviate those challenges?

- What prevents you from making those improvements?

- What's unique about this company as compared to your competitors?

- Describe the communication process. How well does it work?

- What experience have you had working with consultants?

- If you had one message to give your president [CEO, board, manager], what would it be?

- What should I have asked but didn't?

Questions Specific to the Situation

- Why are you considering this project?

- How would you define the scope of this project?

- How will you know that you have gotten a return on the investment of money and time you will spend?

- What will be different as a result of this project?

- What behavioral changes do you expect when this project is successful?

- What specific improvements and changes would you like to see occur?

- How will you measure success?

- What obstacles to success can you predict?

- How will you be involved in this project?

- How will a decision be made about proceeding with this project?

- What's the next step? What do you need from me? Do you want a proposal?

Quick · · · · · · · · · ▶ TIP

If you find that you are doing more than one-half of the talking, you have lost the sale. Stop talking. The meeting is about your potential client—not you. Buyers buy; they are not sold to.

Follow Up After Every Meeting

Get in the habit of following up every meeting with a written note thanking the prospects for their time. Even if you will submit a proposal, dash off a quick note to maintain the momentum of a positive meeting.

Remember that you are still in the exploratory mode. Learn as much as you can at this stage about potential clients, your selling skills, and what you can do better next time.

This chapter helped you determine a need and analyze your competition to land your first work. You have just experienced your first marketing activities. Chapter Nine will expand your market planning.

Quick Start ACTION

Make a Sale to Solve a Problem

Take one hour right now to select three or four potential clients from the list that you created. Begin to complete the research. Stop after 45 minutes. Are you surprised about how much you learned about the clients you selected?

Next, think about how you can connect what you do to what the clients might need. What could be in the initial letter? You are about to go on a sales call—a warm call. Remember that the sales role is the most essential role in all businesses. Without sales, every company will fail. Prepare for this important role.

Imagine that you are sitting across a conference table with one of the clients. How will you open the discussion? What specific words will you use? How will you build rapport? Asking questions is a good way to build rapport. What questions are you comfortable asking? What anecdotes might you be able to tell to demonstrate your expertise? How will you react positively to objections? Remember that your job is to help your potential clients solve a problem. Demonstrate how you can do that, while building a relationship, and you have closed the sale.

Quick Start **LISTS**

Actions I Will Take

Ideas I Have

Questions I Need to Answer

Marketing

9

In this chapter you will

- Create a marketing plan
- Explore creative marketing options on a shoestring budget
- Practice a step-by-step process to write a client proposal
- Develop a client tracking system

What Is Marketing?

Marketing is how you advertise, publicize, or otherwise inform others of your consulting services and products. Your goal is reached when clients purchase your services and products. You may be the best consultant in the world, but until others know about you and purchase what you have to offer, you will not have any business. Obviously you cannot just sit back with your stack of business cards and wait for the phone to ring. You must market your products and services. You must promote yourself.

Your first work may be work that your former employer asked you to complete when you left to begin your consulting business. It may be work that you obtained through members of your network. But you will not be able to depend on people you know to keep you in business. You must reach out to others. The reaching out is your marketing, and your marketing plan will help identify and organize how you will accomplish that.

In Chapter Eight you clarified your niche. Your niche focuses on two things important to your marketing plan. First, it identifies what range of products and services you provide. In other words, are you a generalist or a specialist? Second, it identifies the range of clients you serve. Do you serve a wide market or a narrow market? With this start, you can begin to develop a very simple marketing plan. Volumes and volumes have been written about marketing. Let's condense it all to just the few vital elements you need to get started.

The ABCs of Marketing

Although much has been written about marketing, it can be as easy as ABC:

- Assess your situation.
- Build a client base.
- Contact potential clients.

Assess Your Situation

You started this step in Chapter Eight by examining your consulting business from an internal and external (clients and competition) perspective. When developing a marketing plan, you will explore the discussion about what you offer and to whom in more depth.

A marketing plan requires that you determine where you are today, where you want to be, and what the gap is between these two. For example, you may be offering team-building seminars in which you follow up with coaching to senior leaders. What you really want to be doing is increasing your coaching services and eliminating the team-building seminars. Your marketing plan will take this into consideration and create a road map to that end.

When you explore your customer base, you may discover that 85 percent of your revenues come from government clients. Since they pay lower fees than your private industry clients, you may develop a plan to increase the percentage of private industry clients. And, of course, you should always be aware of what your competition is doing. Creating a marketing plan, however, requires you to dedicate time to a more thorough examination.

Build a Client Base

Once you have assessed your situation, you will use the information to create a marketing plan that targets specific clients or groups of clients. You cannot pursue every potential client, so you need to make difficult decisions in narrowing your client base.

You will place everything into the mix that you have learned in the "A" step about you and your business, your current and potential clients, and your competitors, and look for opportunities. This step will help you identify advertising and publicity options to consider, the marketing media you will use, which clients to target, and what budget you will need.

Contact Potential Clients

This third step, the "C," is actually the follow-through with regard to your marketing plan. This is the sales part of the marketing process.

A marketing plan is a failure if sales do not result. And for consultants, there is only one time to market: *all* the time. You are on and marketing no matter where you are or what you are doing.

Quick · · · · · · · · · · · · ▶ TIP

Marketing is a fascinating subject and critical to your success. If you want to learn more about marketing, contact your local community college, and register for a course. You will not only learn about the marketing basics, but you will also be exposed to ideas you will be able to translate to your consulting business.

Create Your Marketing Plan

This section walks you through the ABCs of marketing to create your first marketing plan.

Your marketing plan must be in writing. A written plan puts discipline into your ideas, enables you to measure success, and provides data for future use.

In Chapter Five you developed a business plan, and one of its sections was devoted to marketing and sales. You can use that information now to initiate the marketing plan.

Review the eight steps presented here. Then use the questions in the next section to build your marketing plan. You will use the information to complete your first annual marketing plan. Have fun! Marketing can be almost as much fun as consulting.

Step 1: Analyze the Present

Market research should be an ongoing activity, so create a systematic method to keep information on client needs up-to-date. If you conduct training as part of your consulting, you can easily gather data through evaluations at the end of the training session. Other methods you might consider are mailed questionnaires, telephone surveys, electronic surveys, or face-to-face interviews.

You want to know how you are perceived in the marketplace, whether you meet your clients' expectations, whether you project the image you desire, and whether you have the reputation you desire.

If you have been in business for over a year, complete this analysis by calling several of your clients to obtain information. For absolutely honest feedback, you will have to conduct anonymous research. If you are just starting out, analyze what you expect to happen over the next 12 months.

Step 2: Clarify Your Strategy

Clarify where your business is heading. You have created your niche in lots of detail. Examine what you stated as your niche in Chapter Eight.

Here you will describe your targeted client base and what you will offer them.

Step 3: Set Measurable 6- to 12-Month Goals

You know the value of goal setting. Set your goals here. Be specific, and write them so that they are measurable. Add time limits to them so you can tell whether you accomplished your goals in a timely manner. Your goals should be results-oriented, not activity-based. Here are some examples:

- Generate $400,000 in new business from July 1 to January 3.
- Acquire three new clients by February 28.
- Acquire one new client in the banking industry by February 28.
- Present at one new conference in the next calendar year.

Step 4: Select Marketing Tactics to Accomplish Your Goals

Tactics are actions you will take to get the word out that you are in business. Marketing experts often divide these tactics into a number of categories. Sometimes marketing is divided into direct and indirect marketing methods. Direct methods include things such as telemarketing, direct mail, magazine advertising, and directory advertising. Indirect marketing methods include such activities as public speaking, seminars, professional affiliations, writing books and articles, public relations, and newsletters.

Marketing is also divided into advertising and promotion. A simple differentiation by some is that advertising is paid for and promotion is free. All of these items qualify as ways to get the word out.

We are not going to concern ourselves about whether your tactics are direct or indirect, advertising or promotion, or any other category. You just need to begin to think about actions you will take to get the word out. Examples include the following:

- Make 25 contacts in the banking industry.

- Submit proposals to at least three new conferences.

- Submit an article to *Banking Today*.

Step 5: Identify Resources

There is always a cost to marketing, whether you take out a four-color full-page ad in a professional journal or write a letter to the editor in your local paper. The ad may cost $10,000 and little of your time if you hire a marketing firm to develop it. The letter may be less than a dollar for a stamp, paper, and an envelope, but six hours of your time to craft it. You must weigh the cost and the benefits to determine whether the investment makes sense to you. How many people will see the ad? How many will see the letter? How many of these people will be members of your niche market? What are the chances of one person responding to your action?

Besides time and money, your resources could also be people. If you are targeting a specific industry, for example, you could have a booth at the industry's conference, take an ad out in its journal, or take someone you know in the industry to lunch to brainstorm ideas for approaching organizations within the industry.

Step 6: Develop an Annual Marketing Activity Calendar

Your marketing activities will be more appealing if you break them down into smaller steps. For example, if your goal is to have one new client in a particular industry within the next six months, the steps to reach that goal might look something like this:

- Ask Wisconsin staff to help identify 10 possible clients by July 5.
- Gather information about the organizations by July 15.
- Brainstorm potential mailing content with Katrina.
- Send first mailing by August 5.
- Complete follow-up calls by August 15.
- Send follow-up mailing with article by September 5.
- Arrange all meetings by October 5.

A layout for your marketing calendar is provided in the next section.

Step 7: Implement Your Plan

If you have developed your plan, you need to be faithful about implementing it. Don't get behind. Even when you're too busy to market, you must market. There will be times when you are busy with a big project and your desire will be to complete the project and skip the marketing. The problem is that when the big project is completed, you may not have another project to be busy with! The time to market is all the time. And the most important time to market is when you are too busy to market.

Step 8: Monitor Your Results and Adjust as Needed

Your plan is your best guess at the moment. You may need to adjust it as changes occur, perhaps in the economy or in the industry you have targeted. Perhaps you targeted small nonprofits and realize that their decision-making process takes too long for you. Therefore, you may need to add some larger for-profits to your mix to decrease the gaps you have between projects.

Whatever is happening, you will use this information as input to the analysis you conduct for your plan next year.

Build Your Marketing Plan

Take some time now to develop a marketing plan for your business.

Step 1: Analyze the Present

How are you perceived in the marketplace?

How do you compare to your competition?

What's happening to your revenue and profits?

How satisfied are your customers?

How do your customers describe you and your performance?

How pleased are you with your image in the marketplace?

Step 2: Clarify Your Strategy

Return to Chapter Eight and review your niche. What strategy will you use to meet those goals?

Describe your targeted client base:

Identify at least seven ways you could reach these clients:

1.

2.

3.

4.

5.

6.

7.

Describe what you will offer these clients:

Identify at least seven things you could tell your clients about these services:

1.

2.

3.

4.

5.

6.

7.

Step 3: Set Measurable 6- to 12-Month Goals

Set at least five measurable goals to build your business (remember to focus on the niche you have described):

1.

2.

3.

4.

5.

Are all five goals measurable?

Have you attached a time to each goal?

Step 4: Select Marketing Tactics to Accomplish Your Goals

You have hundreds of possibilities. Here's a list of nouns to start your creative juices flowing:

business cards	letters	seminars	television
speeches	brochures	conferences	articles
clubs	postcards	network	lunch
email	Internet	directories	news releases
mailings	trade shows	ads	telephone calls
friends	past bosses	books	newsletters
associations	journals	direct mail	logos
stunts	greeting cards	telemarketing	civic organizations
competitors	church	community college	press releases
radio	newspapers	podcasts	pictures
celebrations	congratulations notes	free presentations	testimonials
charity	rumors	holidays	blogs
audiotapes	interviews	awards	webinars
parties	social media	LinkedIn	Facebook Live

Use these nouns to create at least 20 actions that you could complete that will put your name in front of the potential clients you've targeted. Each has many possibilities. For example, if you chose interviews, you could interview 20 industry leaders and publish the results; you could interview a well-respected person at a conference; you could be interviewed by a newspaper about your specialty; you could interview a university professor and send a transcript or a link (with permission, of course) to potential clients; you could interview your clients' customers and include the information in your proposal.

Now it's your turn. Consider all the possibilities, and make up your own. Then decide on at least 15 that are a fit for your clients, your budget, and your personality.

1.

2.

3.

4.

5.

6.

7.

8.

9.

10.

11.

12.

13.

14.

15.

16.

17.

18.

19.

20.

Step 5: Identify Resources

What resources will it take to produce your marketing tactics? Select six of your tactics and estimate how much time and money will be required and who will help you complete your actions.

	Tactic	Who Will Help	Time	Cost
1.				
2.				
3.				
4.				
5.				
6.				

Step 6: Develop an Annual Marketing Activity Calendar

Lay out your plan for the year on the Annual Marketing Activity form.

Annual Marketing Activity

Marketing Activity for (Year)	Jan	Feb	Mar	April	May	June	July	Aug	Sept	Oct	Nov	Dec
Dates												
Cost												
Total Budgeted Costs												

Source: E. Biech, *The New Business of Consulting* (Hoboken, NJ: John Wiley & Sons, 2019).

Step 7: Implement Your Plan

How will you ensure that you complete everything on your calendar every month?

How will you reward yourself for completing your marketing activities?

Quick • • • • • • • • • ▶ TIP

Would you like to have your marketing plan developed for free? Most business schools require marketing students to develop a marketing plan; you could be the recipient. Contact your local college's business school to learn who the marketing instructors are. Then contact them. To ensure that this is not only free but also valuable, do two things. First, allow enough time. Developing a marketing plan will be a long process, usually occurring over almost a full semester. Second, stay involved. Your input will be critical to provide correct data. Your involvement will more than likely increase the enthusiasm of the student. A side benefit may be getting feedback from the professor, as well as hearing ideas from a younger generation.

Step 8: Monitor Your Results and Adjust as Needed

How will you track your results?

How will you know if you need to adjust your plans?

Marketing on a Shoestring Budget

Start-up costs are always more than most of us can predict. What are some ideas for marketing when your revenues are less than you would like?

The process that yields the best results dollar for dollar has already been presented to you. Return to Chapter Eight and review the nine-step plan for landing your first clients. That plan has worked over and over for me. Here are some other ideas:

- If you are planning to attend a conference, submit a proposal to speak. Often the conference sponsor will pay your registration if you speak.

- Make certain you always project a high-quality image through your stationery, business cards, and the letters you write. Cheap cards or sloppy letters may cost much more in lost potential than expensive stationery.

- Cards, letters, and telephone calls cost little as compared to an ad in a journal or the newspaper, and they can be personalized. Quite honestly, save your money—my experience has been that paid ads in journals, newspapers, or magazines don't pull their weight in clients.

- Look for listings in consulting directories that are free or low cost.

- Pass out business cards freely. They are a great bargain, so be sure you have taken the time to word them perfectly and to get the unique look you desire.

- Offer to speak to civic organizations, and be sure to take your business cards and brochures with you.

- Do such a great job that your clients market for you to other organizations or even to other departments in the same organization.

Quick • • • • • • • • • • ▶ TIP

Pay close attention to that last bullet. I returned home from working with a large client last week with four more potential projects in hand: a team-building session, a division strategy session, and two executive-coaching opportunities. All four are from different departments. It is possible that only two or three of the projects will result in a signed contract. Still, doing a great job that leads to additional work is more efficient, less costly, and more certain than taking out an ad or speaking at a trade show. Don't misunderstand me; you need to do many different things for different reasons. But isn't it wonderful that doing what you are supposed to be doing—delivering exceptional services—can do dual duty as marketing too?

What About Internet Marketing?

Internet marketing has its place—as long as you remember that the Internet is good for marketing but not for selling. So you can have a blog, 10,000 followers on LinkedIn, and a regular presence on Facebook, but you still need to find a different way to take the last step. Consultants need to close the sale. It rarely happens on the Internet. Try these thoughts to market your consulting business most effectively and to get yourself in front of decision-makers:

- You probably have a Facebook account, but be sure to also join LinkedIn, where nearly 50 percent of the members have decision-making authority.

- To turn *likes* into *leads* you need to first determine where your audience hangs out; explore Instagram, Twitter, or others.

- Follow at least a dozen people who are thought leaders in consulting or your area of expertise.

- Listen to your audience's issues and concerns and provide value.

- Experiment with premium content that solves your potential clients' problems.

- To be successful, blogging is a weekly commitment. The payoff is that it positions you as the expert, builds a following, and helps to raise your profile.

- Provide a way to drive the traffic from your social media platform to your website. For example, if you advertise on Facebook, focus on getting people to visit your website.

Quick · · · · · · · · ▸ TIP

If you are interested in more writing tips, check out www.rayedwards. com, where you will find blog posts, podcasts, and other resources.

Quick Start ACTION

Grab Attention with Your Headlines

Whether you are posting a blog, creating copy for your website, or creating a mailing piece, it all starts with your headline. We've discussed the importance of focusing on your clients and solving their problems in your content. But if they never get past your headline, they will never know. Practice writing a few headlines here, and then use the checklist that follows to evaluate your headlines.

☐ Does my heading project urgency? You can do that using a time-driven statement. Put time on your side.

☐ Does my heading solve the reader's problem? It needs to be useful and answer the reader's "What's in it for me?" Tune in to radio station WII-FM.

☐ Is my heading personal enough? You can create urgency and answer a problem, but a headline can also create emotion. Do that with emotionally charged words such as: dread, your success, rich, happy, free, or others that are appropriate.

Eliminate adjectives, adverbs, and superlatives. Your headline is the path to the rest of your copy. This quick exercise just helps you start. As Ray Edwards (2016), a copywriter authority, says, "The secret to writing really good headlines . . . is to write a lot of bad ones."

Write Winning Proposals

Proposals will become an integral part of your business development strategy. A proposal may be the last step in the sales process—a statement that summarizes how you have defined and clarified your prospective client's needs. At other times, it may be the first step in a bidding or an introductory process. In either case, it takes time to write a good proposal.

The secret to writing winning proposals is to listen carefully to the client and take good notes or, in the case of a Request for Proposal (RFP), read the information carefully and highlight important information. Give the speaker or the writer back exactly what is asked for. If they ask for a "corrective measures" design and you know that they mean "progressive discipline," use their words anyway. It is amazing to me how many people speak their own language in a proposal instead of the language that the client uses. Maybe your words are more descriptive or more sophisticated, but if the client must translate your proposal before making a decision, your proposal will be near the bottom of the stack. Use their words and you will be surprised at how often you hear clients say, "How did you know? That's exactly what we need!"

Steps to Writing a Proposal

A proposal is simply a statement of who will do what by when and for how much. Follow these steps when writing a proposal:

1. Gather as much information as you can before beginning to write. You might use the questions in Chapter Eight ("What to Ask Potential Clients") to gather some of the data.

2. Plan a structure that will be easy for your clients to find their way around. You may develop your own proposal structure, but the one that is presented here will serve you well. It includes a purpose statement, a description of the situation, a proposed approach, a time line, your qualifications, and the investment (cost) required to complete the plan.

3. Complete each section, writing from your client's perspective, using your client's words and language. Be certain your writing is clear, concise, and descriptive.

4. If the RFP allows it, stay in touch with the client. Sometimes if the RFP is competitive, as is the case in many government RFPs, you are not allowed to speak to the client. If that is not the case, you can clarify information to

avoid making assumptions, gather information you may have missed in earlier conversations, or test any creative options. Certainly you would not want to call every day and make a pest of yourself. Nevertheless, staying in touch, done well, can help to build and maintain rapport and confirm that you care and want to do a good job.

5. Have someone read your proposal to check for typos, clarity, accuracy, and understanding.

6. Don't wait for the last minute. Most proposals are emailed to a central recipient. It would be sad if you waited until the last minute to hit send and their system was down. It's happened to me. Some proposals ask that multiple copies be printed and physically delivered. If that's the case, print the proposal on the best paper that you have. Attach any supplemental material, add a cover to the front, place the requested number of copies in a folder, and either hand-deliver it or send it in an overnight package.

Writing the Proposal

Return to one of the clients you met with in Chapter Eight, and write your first proposal. Use the following guidelines to begin to sketch out your answers and information here.

Cover Page. Include the name of the proposal ("A Proposal Prepared for [Company Name]"), the date, your company name, and contact information.

Purpose Statement. Open with a statement something like this fill-in-the-blank model:

> "This proposal is submitted at the request of **(name), (title), (company)**."
> It includes a description of the situation, a suggested approach, a time line, and the expected investment for the effort.

Write your purpose statement in the space provided:

Description of the situation. Discuss the situation as it currently exists. You may include the current problem, the current need, the desire for the future, or any other pertinent data. Note here some of the specifics of the situation you might include in the proposal:

A proposed approach. This is where you describe exactly what you will do to accomplish the task. What is special about your approach? To make this section easier to understand, you may divide it into subsections and present them in the order that they will occur—for example, Data Gathering, Design Content, Implementation, and Follow-Up. Make some notes about what you might include:

Time line. A time line is exactly what it sounds like. You will need to determine the level of detail you will include. It is always good to include specific dates and milestones. You can list the dates down the left side and the tasks next to the dates. You may also present this information as a graphic picture.

Your qualifications. This is optional. You may choose to include a paragraph about why you are uniquely qualified to complete this project. You may also choose to attach a biographical sketch or your résumé, whichever is appropriate for the industry.

Investment and responsibilities. Use the word *investment* instead of *price* or *cost*. It will help your clients focus on your proposals as something that will benefit them rather than just "cost" them. I also include some of the key responsibilities required to complete the plan in this section. When tied to the investment, it makes an impressive package that says, "Look at all you're getting!" Responsibilities might include materials you will supply and actual work you will complete, such as participant workbooks, decision templates, interviews, specific sessions you will lead, and so on. State travel arrangements also. List the investment and responsibilities for your proposal here:

I close in this way:

> Your investment for (**name of consultation**) will be $X,XXX.00. In addition, travel will be billed at cost.

> The terms of this proposal are effective through (**date**).

> Executive-level references are available.

Attachments. Attachments may be included as an appendix to your proposal. They should be added only if they enhance the proposal. Attachments could include any or all of these items:

- Biographical sketches of the individuals who will work on the project
- A description of your company
- A client list
- Any related materials

Now turn to your computer and begin to enter a draft of your first proposal.

A proposal can also be written in a letter format. If you do that, it will be shorter and perhaps less formal. Use a formal letter format, with subheads within the letter's body. You can find a sample proposal on the website that accompanies my book *The New Business of Consulting*.

Quick · · · · · · · · · · ▶TIP

Keep an electronic and hard copy file of all your proposals. You'll be surprised to see the quality in each improve. In the future, you may even be able to use sections from one proposal for another.

Track Your Clients

"Track my clients?" you might be asking, "Why? I don't have any yet!" But you will! And with all the balls you will need to keep in the air, it's never too soon. Start tracking clients with the first contact you make. You will be surprised at how easily you forget what one client said or when you promised to follow up with a telephone call.

Completing the eight-step marketing plan in this chapter ensures that you have thought through how you will get the word out about your services. It will help you stay focused and committed to ongoing marketing of your services.

Client Contact Log

Organization/ Phone Number	Contact Person	Date	First Contact	Follow-Up	Date	Second Contact	Follow-Up	Date	Third Contact	Follow-Up

Source: *The New Consultant's Quick Start Guide: An Action Plan for Your First Year in Business.* Copyright 2019 by Elaine Biech.

Quick · · · · · · · · · ▶ TIP

Make copies of the Client Contact Log, and place them next to what you see daily or in a file folder. If you have a tendency toward a messy desk, copy the pages on canary yellow or some other bright color or file them in a brightly colored folder. Duplicate this information in your smartphone so that it is with you everywhere you go.

Tips to Become a Better Marketer

The whole point of marketing is to help customers remember you and what you offer. Your business depends on your ability to continually bring in new or repeat business. Here are a few tips to become better at marketing. Implement those that make sense for you.

- Learn to spot an opportunity when you hear it. Then grab it with gusto, and do something about it!

- Begin with a clear message and a clear identity. Who are you and what do you want your clients to remember about you?

- Before you call on a prospective client, obtain a copy of the organizational chart listing all key people, and learn something about the organization's history and current culture.

- Develop name recognition within your industry by speaking at conferences, writing articles and blogs, and volunteering for your professional organization.

- Listen, listen, listen. Listen to what your potential clients say as well as what they do not say during a marketing call.

- Stay in touch with clients as they move from one job to another, and turn reconnecting into a marketing opportunity.

Quick • • • • • • • • • •▶ TIP

Are you landing every proposal and gig you go after? Did you skip the preceding tips because you think you have marketing under control? Think again. Perhaps your rates are too low. You do not want to gain a reputation of the "low bidder." Save bargains for department stores.

- Develop relationships with those people whom you believe will be the next leaders of the organization.

- Market all the time. Make marketing a mindset.

- Write a book. Authoring a book gives you respect, credibility, and an increased level of trust in your expertise. A book can be your giant business card.

Remember that no amount of marketing will turn your business into a cash machine. You still need to do the work.

Quick Start **LISTS**

Actions I Will Take

Ideas I Have

Questions I Need to Answer

Surviving the First Year

10

In this chapter you will

- Identify a plan to take care of your mental and physical health
- Establish a plan to manage your time
- Establish good habits for managing a business
- Establish a plan to balance your life
- Develop a personal ethics statement for operating your business

Take Care of Your Health

Many people I meet think of consulting as an exciting, high-powered career: flying from coast to coast, meeting with publishers in San Francisco and executives in New York City, staying at the Madison in Washington, D.C., or the Ritz Carlton in Dallas, eating at a coffee shop in Seattle. I am paid well, dress well, land large contracts, and hobnob with the influential. But that's only the first layer.

My friends know what my life is really like: up at 4:00 a.m. to catch a flight for a noon meeting, spending six hours in an airport because of delayed flights, canceling dinner plans, and finally arriving home at midnight. It is also about eating poorly prepared restaurant food, writing proposals until the wee hours of the morning, and losing a contract due to a technicality. Most of all, it is about long hours.

You do have the freedom to set your own schedule—but often those hours are long. You will make enough money to eat well. And it will take a concerted effort to do so when you're on the road.

We've touched on taking care of your health in Chapters Two and Seven. That demonstrates the importance. You can't be a good entrepreneur and consultant if you are not healthy. Identify how you will continue to maintain a healthy lifestyle by answering these questions:

What was your exercise routine before becoming a consultant? (or What is the ideal exercise routine you'd like to start?) How will you ensure that you get regular exercise?

What eating habits do you want to maintain? What new eating habits do you want to start? How will you do this while traveling?

What kinds of things have caused stress for you in the past? What stress reducers have you used that work? What is your plan to prevent stress as a consultant?

Manage Your Time

We all have exactly 24 hours in every day. And while we all talk about saving time, we really cannot. Time continues to march on. We can't save it. We can, however, shave time. Here are some time-shaving tips for you. Then we'll show you how to identify your greatest time wasters.

The Big Jobs

Work on several large projects rather than dozens of small projects. You use a great deal of time traveling from one client to another, remembering names, and getting up to speed on the project. This means that you must use a marketing strategy that ensures that you acquire larger projects rather than smaller ones.

I have always maintained that focusing on large organizations is good for new consultants. Fortune 500 clients have always been my base. They have more available work, greater ability to pay, and more chances for repeat work. They will be a respected addition to your client list and it will likely take you less time to land a gig with them. Go after the big fish; it takes the same amount of time to bait the hook.

Do the Hardest First

Do some tasks challenge you more than others? Do you sometimes feel uncomfortable? Do you feel unqualified to complete an action? Well, get used to it. You will be expected to do many things that are not easy. Don't assume that others have an easy time with the things you struggle with. We all do everything for the first time, sometime!

Chances are very good that the thing you need to do that is uncomfortable and difficult is one of the most important things you need to do. Suck it up. Just do it.

Do the hardest thing first. Imagine how good you will feel when the hardest one is over for the day.

Invoice Ease

Chasing cash flow may be one of your most precarious dilemmas. Timely invoicing is the only solution. In order to be paid you must invoice your clients in a timely manner. The same day isn't too soon. In the beginning, it is likely that you will be the one who invoices your clients. Keep an invoice template on your computer for clients who will incur repeat billings. When it's time to bill them, simply complete the date and the invoice amount and print it or email it.

Keep a generic template for all the rest of your clients. Again, it saves the time of starting a new one each time. Be sure to check the financial software your accountant recommended. It is likely to have a form for you to use. Even so, I'd customize it, adding your logo and unique typeface so that it looks more professional.

Tickler Files

Keep tickler files by month in your desk drawer or on your computer desktop. Place items in them that need attention in each particular month. When you open the file for each month, you will be reminded of what needs to be completed. For example, when I pull the May file, I have written items under both personal and business. Personal: Annual checkup, call to initiate lawn mowing, and air conditioner checkup. Business: Renew lease, submit incorporation minutes, and pay annual office property taxes. On the inside of that folder I also have a list of everyone I know who has a birthday in May.

As you continue to consult, you will acquire your own time shavers. To truly identify how you spend your time, you will need to keep a Time Management Log, like the one shown here. The log will give you the data you need to identify where you could manage your time better. Keep the log for a week or two. You may be very surprised at where your time goes.

For example, last week I spoke with a consulting colleague. She is also an adjunct professor. After tracking her time, she was surprised at how much time she spent on her duties as a professor and even more surprised when she figured out how little she was being paid for her time.

As another example, the last time I kept a time log, I was surprised to learn that when I am in the office, I spend almost half of my time on the telephone, either talking or calling and leaving messages for people who aren't available. Related to this, I found that waiting for someone to return my call was delaying the start of some projects. Was it any wonder that I could not get proposals written while I was in the office? I initiated two things as a result of reviewing this information. First, I work out of my home office when I have large projects such as proposals or writing a book. Second, I have my staff tell people when I will be available for phone calls—Thursday between 10:00 a.m. and noon, for example. It has shaved quite a bit of time for me and I am able to complete my priorities in a more timely manner.

Time-Management Log

Name: _____   Date: _____

Hour	15-Minute Intervals					Daily Summaries

List task categories after each letter code (meetings, telephone calls, marketing, consulting, administration, planning, and so forth). Then put the corresponding letter into the block that was dominated by each task. Do not allow more than one hour to pass before updating this log. Multiply the number of blocks by 15 minutes to find out how much time was spent on each task.

Hour (15-Minute Intervals):

- 12:00 a.m.
- 1:00 a.m.
- 2:00 a.m.
- 3:00 a.m.
- 4:00 a.m.
- 5:00 a.m.
- 6:00 a.m.
- 7:00 a.m.
- 8:00 a.m.
- 9:00 a.m.
- 10:00 a.m.
- 11:00 a.m.
- 12:00 p.m.
- 1:00 p.m.
- 2:00 p.m.
- 3:00 p.m.
- 4:00 p.m.
- 5:00 p.m.
- 6:00 p.m.
- 7:00 p.m.
- 8:00 p.m.
- 9:00 p.m.
- 10:00 p.m.
- 11:00 p.m.

Code	Task	#	Total Time
A.	_____	____ × 15 =	____
B.	_____	____ × 15 =	____
C.	_____	____ × 15 =	____
D.	_____	____ × 15 =	____
E.	_____	____ × 15 =	____
F.	_____	____ × 15	____
G.	_____	____ × 15 =	____
H.	_____	____ × 15 =	____
I.	_____	____ × 15 =	____
J.	_____	____ × 15 =	____

Source: The New Consultant's Quick Start Guide: An Action Plan for Your First Year in Business. Copyright 2019 by Elaine Biech.

Looking for more time? You'll never find time for everything. You must make it. The following list of time management techniques will not be new to you. But remind yourself of those that you could practice more diligently. Check the box next to the ones you could do better:

- ☐ Set your priorities first thing in the morning or the last thing at night for the next day.

- ☐ Do your top A priorities first.

- ☐ Tackle large projects in stages.

- ☐ Identify your best times, that is, your best time for writing, best time to make telephone calls, and so forth.

- ☐ Use your waiting and travel time productively: make lists, listen to podcasts, balance your checkbook.

- ☐ Use your tablet, smartphone, or carry notecards or a small notebook to list ideas or reminders.

- ☐ Handle each piece of paper only once.

- ☐ Have a place for everything.

- ☐ Set deadlines.

- ☐ Make decisions in a timely way. Indecision is a time thief.

- ☐ Always ask, "Is this the best use of my time right now?"

- ☐ Set a schedule, and stick to it.

- ☐ Take short breaks often.

- ☐ Have something to do when you're put on hold.

- ☐ Become a great communicator.

- ☐ Minimize interruptions.

As a business owner, time is your most precious resource. Manage it well, and guard it jealously. Once it is gone, you will never get it back.

Quick ‥‥‥‥‥► TIP

Before you leave this section, pull out your planner or calendar, and do a quick assessment on how you have spent your time so far this week. What does it tell you? Are you doing the things that will get you to the goals you identified in Chapter Two? What changes might you make? Do you have any bad habits that will be difficult to overcome? For example, do you like to talk on the phone, do you spend more time on Facebook than you want, or do you procrastinate when faced with big projects?

Establish Good Business Habits

What better time to start new habits—good habits—than when starting a business? Good habits will make your business run more smoothly, ensuring you are making the best use of your time. They may seem like little things, but they will turn up as critical sooner or later. New habits can begin when you want them to begin. Here are a few that are worth starting now.

The Basics

- Create a good filing system. Chapter Seven addressed the good filing habits you could initiate. Go back to that chapter, and review them before reading about other good habits.

- Add copyrights to all original documents. More than once I've found my original work floating around in an organization or being used by another consultant. I have always been willing to share, but I like to be asked. If I have put my copyright on something, I know there was some effort expended in cutting it off, whiting it out, or taping over it. If your integrity is ever questioned, a dated copyright on your material protects you and your work.

- Date everything. Someday you will look through a file, find just what you wanted, and pat yourself on the back for a good filing system, only to find out that the survey was dated August—that's it. Just "August." August what? The most important number has been left off. It's happened to me many more times than I care to mention.

Financial Advice

- Get comfortable with variations in revenue. Begin to track trends and plan ahead for the lean months.

- Manage your cash flow. It's more important than profit.

- Bill all completed work immediately. One of the best favors you can do for your cash flow is to invoice your client within 24 hours of completing the project. Your bank statement will thank you.

- Track expenses carefully with either an app or a simple filing system for paper receipts. No, your pockets do not qualify as a good filing system.

- Be sure you are charging what you are worth. If not, make adjustments sooner rather than putting it off.

- Give your clients a six-month advance notice before changing your fee structure.

Client Counsel

- Never stop marketing—especially when you are too busy to market.

- Manage client relationships. Your project will end, but the relationship should continue.

- Make follow-up with clients your top priority. Seems logical, doesn't it? You will be surprised at how many things can come between you and a simple return telephone call. Time gets away from me in the afternoon. All too soon it's 12:30, whoops! 5:30 in London—too late to return that call. Don't let it happen.

- Avoid dependency on one client. Plan to have no more than 30 percent of your work from one client.

- Say no to work that doesn't fit your niche—unless—yes there is always an "it depends," isn't there? In this case, if you see an opportunity where you can add value and learn something that you've wanted to learn or if you think it might lead to something else in the organization, I'd say "yes."

- Get comfortable with losing clients, proposal bids, and prospects. You don't want all the business—just the best business.

Finally, step into your new role with an abundant mindset. There is plenty of work for everyone. Don't hesitate to share what you know with others. Share your time and resources with others. It will benefit the entire world. What good habits do you want to start with this business? List them here.

Delight Your Clients

I love the word *delight*. It has such a pleasant, happy, joyful ring and it conjures up a client that is pleased and will hire you again or will refer you to others. How can you delight your clients this first year? Try a few of these suggestions and add more of your own.

- **Go the extra mile.** Your clients will notice when you provide more than you promise.

- **Surprise them.** If you hear someone talking about the latest best-seller, order a copy and give it as a surprise gift.

- **Be generous.** I used to say, "the more you give, the more you get," but that sounds selfish and it is not what I ever meant. I find that the more I give, the more we all grow—as professionals and as human beings.

- **Acknowledge them.** When those on the client's team have contributed to the project, be sure they are recognized.

- **Send a card.** Find a reason to send greeting cards—no, not an ecard, a paper card for holidays that cards aren't usually associated with, such as Halloween, Independence Day, Cinco de Mayo, First Day of Spring, Groundhog Day, or others.

- **Celebrate.** Find a silly reason to celebrate. For example, did you know that January 8 is Clean Off Your Desk Day? Or that June 1 is National Donut Day? Those two should give you a couple of ideas.

- **Add value.** Data geeks use the term proof of value to show that AI or big data provides results. You can deliver proof of value, too, when you demonstrate results. Track data and qualitative examples. Share them with your clients.

- **Show your passion.** Your excitement and desire to do what you love will rub off on your clients and they will be delighted to be working with you.

- **Build trust.** Building trust does not mean that you are the expert all the time, although your expertise is one reason your clients hired you. You will also build trust based on your transparency (I don't know but I will find out), accuracy (I've confirmed the data is correct), and the choices you make about dependability and candor. Start with a solid foundation and build the trust every day.

Balance Your Life

One of the most challenging aspects of being a consultant is finding balance. While I do not profess to have the answer, I do have some suggestions to offer.

Identify Any Imbalance

Identify what seems to be out of balance in your life. How do you know? Geoff Bellman, author of *The Consultant's Calling* (2002), uses this exercise in his sessions. List three things you value most in your life. Write them here:

1.

2.

3.

Now scan your checkbook, credit card statement, and your calendar. Do your checkbook credit card statement, and calendar indicate that those are the most valuable things in your life? If not, determine what you can do about it. Write your ideas here.

Make Your Own Rules

Make up rules that help you maintain your balance. Create rules that help put your business in perspective. Tell yourself, "If it's not done by 6:00 p.m., it can wait until tomorrow." I sometimes spend too much time fretting about a decision on the horizon that won't occur for days, weeks, or months. I have learned to put it out of my mind by setting a date with myself: "I'll think about that on November 13," and then I do. Perhaps your rule is, "My number one business rule is to spend Saturday morning with my children."

What rules can you make to help you add more balance to your life? List two here:

1.

2.

Enjoy the Doing

Don't overload yourself so much that you miss the fun in the doing. If you like consulting, enjoy all of it. Much of the pleasure is in the doing. Another part of enjoying what you are doing is to examine whether our thoughts are positive or negative—I enjoy what I am doing; I don't enjoy it. I will do what I love; too many roadblocks prevent me from doing what I love. I will work with this client; this client will never hire me.

Every thought that you have leads you one way or another down your path to doing what you love. You are the only one who can make that choice. And yes, of course, I am not so naïve as to think that you will not encounter potholes and barriers along the way. You will. But how you deal with setbacks is one sign of an entrepreneur. You need to continue to make the right choices along your journey.

Are you enjoying what you are doing? How will you ensure that you enjoy all of it? How will you address problems along the way?

Take Time Off

It's important to take a break from your business. Go on a vacation. Go to a day spa. Spend an afternoon reading a book. Visit a state park. Take your niece on a picnic. Go for a walk around the block.

How do you plan to take time off this year?

Identify Other Interests

Join an investment club. Learn golf. Try embroidery. Fly a kite. Collect something. Visit an antique store. Go hiking. Read catalogues. Learn to paint. Take a gourmet cooking class. Write poetry. Work crossword puzzles. Refurbish a classic car. Study your heritage. Go for walks. Develop your family tree. Write a letter. Plan a trip with your spouse, your children, your parents, or a friend.

List five things here you've always wanted to try.

1.

2.

3.

4.

5.

Take Advantage of Being Your Own Boss

If you work at home, find ways and times to get away from it all. Go for a walk; work out at the gym a couple of days each week; eat lunch in your backyard. If you work in an office, stay home a couple of days each month and work on your deck.

How can you take advantage of being your own boss?

Manage Your Balance

Issues of balance are more acute during transitions. So if you are going through your transition to consulting, you should know what to expect.

How might balance shift initially in the various areas of your life, and what do you want to do to maintain balance?

Social?

Family?

Relationships?

Spiritual?

Business?

Education?

Financial?

Others?

In some respects, the issue of balance in life is one of time management. You must prioritize deliberately, based on what you want out of life—what you value.

Did You Hear the One About the Consultant . . . ?

These days there are almost as many consultant jokes as lawyer jokes. As a consultant, your principles are always on the line. What do you stand for?

Why Ethics?

I was a relatively new consultant from the Midwest who had just landed a sales call with my first big East Coast company. I was certain that one of the reasons I had been invited to this meeting was that my price was a lot lower than the East Coast consulting companies I was bidding against. I knew that two of them were huge consulting groups with thousands of employees. I had sent my proposal ahead of the meeting, in which I quoted my price for the six-month-long project. As the discussions were wrapping up, I was shocked to hear the director of training say, "So what's your real price?" I was speechless. That was probably a good thing or I would have tripped over my own words. I just stared at him because no one had ever said that to me.

That wasn't the last time my pricing was tested. I believe it is completely unethical to quote one price and then acquiesce when the organization says, we don't have that in the budget; could you do it for less? Gee, if you can do it for $13,000, why did you quote $19,000? Are you scamming them? Well, no. We know that pricing isn't a precise science. And it is tempting to accept a lower price when you don't have a gig lined up for next month. Still, every consultant who does that gives consulting a bad name.

What can you do? If you truly believe in your rate, stick to your price. I have never had a situation when the money wasn't found someplace. Declaring that they don't have sufficient funds usually means they had low expectations and that they don't have sufficient funds—*yet*. If they want you, they will find the money. Your second option is to offer to cut back on services: fewer interviews, no off-site presentation, fewer coaching sessions, or other things that might be in your proposal. Don't allow a potential client to ruin your reputation by asking you to do something unethical!

Your clients will hire you, and much of their decision is based on how much they want to work with you. Your reputation is on the line with every project. By the way, the big East Coast company paid my price and we worked together for more than 10 years.

On occasion, you will be faced with making a decision that borders on being unethical. These decisions are rarely black and white, rarely pitting good with bad. Instead, they toy with the gray area in the middle. For example, one of the executives I am currently working with has asked me to spend an hour or two talking about his plans for the future when he leaves the organization. It will occur in the middle of an eight-hour day for which the organization is paying me. Yes, it's a deplorable hourly rate, the only way our federal government bids. I've suggested we talk over lunch, but he is not available. The executive is in charge of the contract and should know better. The organization expects to pay for eight hours. What should I do?

Another ethics dilemma often occurs when I am coaching a leader in a company. The organization has hired me to help the leader, so the company is paying my fee. On occasion, if my coaching is helpful to the employee, it may be detrimental to the organization—such as instances when leaving the company is the best thing for the employee. Every situation is different, but the question is still the same. What should I do?

Although it is not always possible, it is still helpful to think about the options that lead to the right decision. Developing your personal ethics statement can help you forecast what might occur and what best matches your principles.

Developing a Personal Ethics Statement

A personal ethics statement can help you make decisions. I know that once I wrote my statement, I was able to make decisions about those gray areas much easier. And, by the way, clients notice.

Begin to identify a list of the ethical standards you will uphold as a consultant. This list will grow as your business grows. Your ethics should be those things you feel deeply about and believe are the foundation of who you are.

You might create ethical statements around some of the following:

- The kinds of projects you will accept
- How you use your time
- The quality of your work
- The kinds of organizations you will work with
- Delivery of services

- How you treat your clients

- Continuous improvement issues

- Goals for your clients

- Work standards

- Pricing

- How you deal with expenses

- Anything else you feel strongly about

Begin your statement of ethics here. Transfer it to a place where you will see it regularly. Update it as you and your business grow. Remind yourself every day that when your name is on the door, your ethics are on the line.

Although this book focuses on developing a consulting practice, you must be certain to work toward a balanced life as well.

Quick Start **LISTS**

Actions I Will Take

Ideas I Have

Questions I Need to Answer

So, Now What? Year Two and Beyond

11

In this chapter you will

- Assess your progress
- Plan your next steps

Assess Your Progress

Congratulations! You've made it though your first year of consulting. And if you are reading this chapter, you must be considering moving forward. Great!

Let's assess your progress and plan your next steps. Take some time to answer the following questions, which address your first year in consulting.

Is consulting all that you had dreamed it would be? Why or why not?

How satisfied do you think your clients are? How do you know?

How successful have you been financially?

How much fun are you having?

Now compare your responses to some of these thoughts:

Is consulting all that you dreamed it would be? People often see consulting as a dream job. You most likely have learned the realities of the business. Travel isn't as glamorous as it first appears. Working at home without someone to talk to gets lonely, and clients who don't pay their bills in a timely manner can wreak havoc on your savings account. All in all, though, it is a great way to make a living. You have freedom and flexibility to do it your way. Your first year is always the most difficult. There is so much to learn! I hope you made some money and had some fun, too.

How satisfied do you think your clients are? How do you know? If you intend to continue consulting, you need lots of satisfied customers who will continue to use you, will recommend you to other clients, and will sing your praises. You have probably had conversations with many of them asking about your services and what you could do better. Stay in touch with all these clients. Create mailing lists—electronic, as well as a postal mail list—so that you can send group emails or run labels easily to keep them informed of what you are doing. These clients will be your customer base for the rest of the time you are in business. Some will use you again and again. Some will refer you over and over to many others.

How successful have you been financially? How are you doing? You should be able to begin to pay back some of those loans you took out during year one. If not, it might be time to take a hard look at your numbers. Are expenses higher than you anticipated? Is that due to not having all the data for good estimates? Or are you being more extravagant than a start-up company should be? In any case, there is an important lesson for you. If expenses are not higher, is income lower than you projected? Why is that? How would you rate your marketing efforts? Are you marketing "all the time"? You need to make money to stay in business.

How much fun are you having? Or, as my friend Pam says, "Are we having fun yet?" Remember my comment in Chapter One: "We should not get up to go to work in the morning. We should be able to get up and go to play!" Consulting can be play. The transition to get there may be difficult for everyone involved. Are you still going through some of the transition trials? If so, do you see an end in sight? Are the people around you having fun, too? Do you hear pride in their voices when they discuss what you are doing? Pay attention to that balance because it's critical. Is consulting as much fun as you expected?

Quick Start ACTION

Review Your First Year with Your Family

It's time to sit down and have a frank discussion with your spouse, significant other, roommate, or family. Right now, without hesitation, block out time on your calendar for that discussion. Use these questions to guide your discussion:

- How satisfied have we been with the past year's arrangements?

- What has worked well this past year?

- How would each of us rate the following?

  - Communication?

  - Financial situation?

  - Social time?

- Personal time?

- Work time?

- What has been the most difficult change?

- How well have we adjusted to the office arrangements?

- What's been the most satisfying for each of us?

- How much fun are we all having?

- Have we had enough time together? Too much?

- What can we do better next year? How will we know it's better?

Plan Your Next Steps

Spend time thinking about your next steps. Let's examine them from your professional perspective, your financial perspective, and your personal perspective.

Professional

You will most likely learn more during your first year of consulting than at almost any other time in your life. This past year has also been a time that tested your capabilities as they have never been tested before. Go back and read Chapter One in this guide. You might be surprised at the new meaning that all of those words have now.

Review this list of attributes of successful consultants. Give yourself a grade for each. Decide how you can leverage the A's and B's to improve the C's and D's. How can your mentor help you? You do have a mentor, right?

☐ Passionate

☐ Generous

☐ Confident

☐ Disciplined

- ☐ Competitive

- ☐ Tenacious

- ☐ Accountable for all my actions

- ☐ Motivated self-starter (takes initiative)

- ☐ Exudes integrity

- ☐ Positive thinker

- ☐ Long-term mindset

- ☐ Lifelong learner

- ☐ Trustworthy

- ☐ Believes excellence isn't optional

- ☐ Embraces failure

- ☐ Willing to take risks

What clues do these attributes give you about what you need to improve? You might wonder about "embraces failure." Failure means that you are out there on the edge and trying new things. You need to live a bit beyond your comfort zone in order to learn and grow. Failing forces us to try other things. Besides, F-A-I-L simply stands for "Find Another Ingenious Lead." If you are achieving all your goals, you probably aren't setting them high enough. You could achieve more by setting more difficult goals and failing a few times. Failure is just another word for try, try again.

Related to failure is taking risks. Entrepreneurs know the value of taking risks. Don't get too comfortable and don't feel as if you need to get everything under control. I love the quote by racecar driver Mario Andretti: "If you have everything under control, you're not moving fast enough." This is true with your consulting career. How fast are you moving?

What do you still need to learn this year about running your business? Do you need to know more about organizing yourself and your office? If you knew more about marketing, would that task be more fun? How about finance? Are you as good at crunching those numbers and knowing what they are telling you? How about process improvement? Do you know how to determine the root cause when something goes wrong and address that to prevent it from occurring again? How are your administrative skills? Thinking about getting some help so that you can be more productive on other things? What is your plan for learning what you need?

You owe it to your clients to stay on top of all that is happening in the field. What did you do this past year to maintain your skills, knowledge, and expertise? What will you do next year? What professional organizations will you join? What professional journals will you read? What conferences will you attend?

How well have you maintained your network of professionals for support and growth? What can you do this next year to give your network a boost?

Financial

Take a good look at your numbers for the past year and determine the following:

- Was your income as high as you projected?
- Were your expenses at the level you projected?
- Did you have lots of highs and lows over the year?
- Were you able to pay yourself the salary you planned?

Profit

Profit is the reason businesses exist, and it doesn't just happen; you must plan for it. (Remember your business plan?) As a good business owner, you should plan to have more profits than if you simply put that same investment away and let it grow interest. How much is a good profit? Can you make 10 percent interest by investing your money with your financial planner? Probably pretty close. Therefore, 10 percent may be an acceptable small stretch and a good place to begin.

You should consider your first year in business a smashing success if you were able to pay yourself the salary you intended. Your second year, however, should find you planning for a profit. Your goal should be to pay yourself a good salary and in addition begin to have a 10 to 30 percent profit on top of that every year. Profit is what is left over after all the expenses are paid. You will pay taxes on that profit.

How do you begin to manage your business to increase profits? There are many things that go into the formula. To increase profits, you can:

- Increase the number of billable days

- Increase the price of your services

- Decrease expenses

    You also must consider the following:

- If you increase your price, will you continue to sell as much?

- How will your clients respond to a higher price?

- Could you increase quality or the value added for a client to justify a higher price?

- How do your prices compare now to your competitors' prices?

Review Your Niche

How did you do with your marketing this year? Could you have done more to get the word out about you and the services you offer? Perhaps you should broaden your niche. How could you do that? Here are some ways:

- You could broaden the services and products you offer to existing clients.

- You could attract new customers—perhaps broadening the customer base niche that you have defined.

- You could expand your line of products and services. Any of the following could become legitimate consulting profit centers:

  - Write a newsletter for profit (rather than as a marketing tool).

  - Write and sell a book, though my experience is that it will be a good tool to increase your fee or enhance your marketing, but it won't make money on its own.

  - Host public seminars.

  - Produce and sell directories.

  - Become a keynote speaker. Join the National Speakers Association (NSA) if this is one of your choices.

  - Develop and teach an online course.

In the end, there are really only two things you can do differently to change your financial situation:

- Bring in more income.

- Allow fewer expenses.

But you have a multitude of ways to do both.

First-year businesses rarely produce a profit because there is always some reason you need to plow your money back into the business. You should plan for a profit during your second year, though. The first thing you may want to do is examine how you are charging. Are you just selling your time? Could you sell the value to your clients? How will you increase profits next year?

Personal

How well have you taken care of yourself? How well did you take care of your mental and physical health? Were you able to get the same exercise that you enjoyed before you became a consultant? How's your stress level? Were you able to keep all the balls in the air and still feel sane? How's the diet? If you had a home office, were you able to resist the refrigerator? What are your plans for next year?

How did you do at managing your time? Did you work only a few weekends? That's great. Did you take a family vacation this year? If not, are you planning one soon? What other time management plans do you want to try?

Have you been able to maintain a balance? Have you found time for friends, family, and hobbies, in addition to time for work? How would you change that balance if you could?

Have you enjoyed the benefits of being your own boss? Perhaps you were able to attend your daughter's first dance recital at three in the afternoon. Perhaps you were able to work 10 p.m. to midnight when no one bothers you and sleep in the next day. Perhaps you've been able to read your professional journals in the neighborhood park. Perhaps you've been able to spend all afternoon reading business books and sipping coffee in your local bookstore. How can you take greater advantage of the benefits of being your own boss next year?

Have you seen how the financial gains can support you and your family? Did you provide all the benefits that you would have had if you were someone's employee? If not, this is the time to review them and decide what you want to do. Did your retirement contribution suffer because you were starting your business? Now is the time to boost that up. What's your plan?

Bring It All Together

I've presented several new directions for you to consider. How do you bring it all together? First go back to Chapter Two and examine your goals. Are you closer to your goals than you were a year ago? Have your goals changed? How will new or adjusted goals affect your consulting business? Explain it here.

Assuming you will continue your consulting business, begin to complete the following questions and tasks. Check off each as you complete it:

☐ Review all your financial statements. Examine your revenue projections for next year, your budget, and your expense records. What changes will you make for next year?

☐ Evaluate your cash flow situation. Do you bill immediately on completion of a project? Do your clients pay you in a timely manner? If this is less than satisfactory, develop a process that will increase the chances of their paying you faster. Describe the process you will use next year.

☐ Review your pricing structure. Should you charge more? Less? Should you have different levels of pricing for different clients? For different services? Should you price by the project instead of the day? Do you show your clients the value they receive? Should you expand your services or your products? Make a decision about your pricing structure for next year.

☐ Review your business plan. Although you should have referred to it regularly throughout the year, now study it more carefully. Are you wiser about your competition than you were last year? What do you still need to learn? Rate your progress on your goals. What new goals will you set for next year?

☐ Review your relationships with your accountant, attorney, banker, and insurance representative. Are you satisfied? What services would you like that you are not receiving? Is it time to meet with any of them to evaluate services? What changes do you want next year?

☐ Review your client relationships. Are your clients beginning to refer you to other clients? Have you completed all projects with high marks of satisfaction? If you had any difficulties, are you satisfied that you have dealt with the root cause to ensure it doesn't occur again? What will you do differently next year?

☐ Review your marketing plan. Did you achieve your goals? What will you change for next year? Will you increase your marketing budget? Which clients can you tap for referrals? How will you market your business differently next year?

☐ Review the specific marketing tactics you are using. How can you leverage your knowledge? Are you blogging regularly? Is it time that you wrote and published a book?

☐ Review how you can productize your intellectual property. Do you conduct strategic planning or use assessments? Could you name them and charge for them along with your services? For example, if you provide team building could you name the questionnaire that clients complete "Team Tracker" and charge for it? Could you design and sell an online course based on the services you provide?

☐ Review the location of your office. Are you still satisfied? Running out of room? Wearing out your welcome at home? Is your business intruding on your home life? Is your home life intruding on your business? Is the image of working out of your house an issue for your clients? For you? If you move, how will you ensure a smooth transition? Where will your office be located next year?

☐ How about employees? Are you considering hiring them now? Who? To fulfill what roles? Where will they work? Where will you find them? When will you hire them? Will they be full time or part time? Will they be employees or subcontractors? How will you support the added expense? Be sure to check the Internal Revenue Service's independent contractor guidelines and discuss this with your attorney. How will you make this a reality next year?

☐ Look far out to five or 10 years from now. What do you see yourself doing? How will your consulting practice look at that time? How and when will you leave the business? Sell it? Leave it to your child? Slip out the back door? What can you do next year to move in the direction of your future 10 years from now?

☐ Did you take care of yourself this year? Remember that your business is nothing without you. You are the business. How well did you manage your time, deal with stress, take care of your health? How well did you balance your life? What will you do differently next year?

☐ Are you ready to make changes that will boost you into your next year? Even if you are comfortable where you are today, you won't know all that you can accomplish if you don't try something else. I like the quote by Zayn Malik, "There comes a day when you realize turning the page is the best feeling in the world, because you realize there is so much more to the book than the page you were stuck on." Don't get stuck on a comfortable page.

Quick Start ACTION

Review Your First Year with a Colleague

Contact a member of your network to schedule a time when this person will go over your responses with you. Ask for input about your answers for next year.

This chapter is a review of your progress to date. It should have given you reason to pause and consider what you did well, what needs improvement, and what you might do differently next year.

Consulting is a challenging yet rewarding profession. You may work harder than you ever have before, yet love the work more than any other. It can be risky, but the payoffs are worth it.

ebb's 13 Truths to Ponder

I introduced ebb's 13 Truths to the ebb associates fledgling staff in 1990 at our newly opened Norfolk office. These truths have served me, ebb associates, and the consultants I coach well over the years. The Truths are a good way to wrap up this book.

As I analyze them I am fascinated to discover that all of them are related to advice about marketing—some more directly than others! Let's take a look.

1. **You Need Clients More Than They Need You.** This is the entire purpose of marketing and selling your consulting services. You need clients or you will not be in business very long. Sometimes I talk to consultants who are certain that they have the magic elixir to solve all clients' needs. That kind of attitude will get you in trouble and in debt. Your marketing should be focused on how you can serve your clients. Help your clients and they will help you with your marketing.

2. **Listening Is Imperative.** Throughout the book I suggested behaviors and attributes that will make you a successful consultant. "Listening" was repeated again and again. Listening is the least expensive and most important marketing tool you have at your disposal. The payoff is immeasurable.

When I've asked clients "What is the most important factor in a relationship with a consultant?" the most common response is, "Take time to understand our needs." I have often thought that every organization should have an official listener on staff. And when they do not, I serve that purpose.

3. **Do Your Homework.** Spend time finding out about your clients before you meet with them and then don't ever stop learning. Everything that you learn will help you in two ways. Clients begin to trust you when they realize you have put effort into researching them. First, it is your responsibility to do the best job possible for your clients. You can't if you do not do your homework. Second, everything you learn about your clients personally and about the organization is potential input into your next marketing idea. Keep your ears and eyes wide open and do your homework. Consulting is all about doing your homework.

4. **You Must Believe In What You Do.** If you think of marketing and selling as crass and pushy—stop! If you believe in what you do, and truly believe that you add value for your clients, you will see selling as providing assistance and help to your clients. Everyone has a great opening line, but the real test is behind the scenes and how you help clients during the difficult times. Believing in what you do will come across sincerely in your work and in your marketing message.

5. **The More Specialized You Are, the More Difficult It Is to Obtain Business; the More Generalized You Are, the Less Credible You'll Be to Potential Clients.** This has always been a dilemma for consultants. If you narrow your niche too much it may be difficult to find clients who require your specific services. On the other hand if you claim to be able to do everything, your clients will wonder about your credibility. Finding the right mix so that what you offer is what your clients need is the key.

6. **The Time to Market Is All the Time.** You simply cannot stop marketing. You are selling you and the image you project. That means you are "on" all the time. When you attend a community gathering or a service organization meeting, when you meet your children's teachers and friends, and when you are shopping or having your oil changed. You are marketing all the time. The receptionist you were short with last week may be this week's gatekeeper who will not let you in to see his boss. Remember you are your own marketing billboard.

7. **The Most Important Time to Market Is When You're Too Busy to Do So.** You are working on the biggest contract you've ever landed. You have lists of

marketing activities to do, but the current client is counting on you and that marketing stuff seems so nebulous. Besides, you don't know if anything will come of it anyway. Well, without completing the marketing activities, nothing will come of it for sure. If you do not market yourself today when you are too busy to market, you will soon have plenty of time to market—all of it! Chapter 9 presents a simplified marketing planning tool. Don't skip it.

8. **A Billable Day Is a Billable Day.** Once a day is gone you can never have it back. If you are selling products and you stop selling for the day, you may be able to sell twice as many products the next day. But you are selling a service and that service is embodied in you. You can't sell two days' worth of yourself on the same day. This does not suggest that you should be billable full time. It simply admonishes you to use your time wisely. And a very important part of that wise time use is marketing. Your billable time is critical to keep the cash flowing. And your marketing efforts ensure that your billable time is maximized.

9. **If You're in It for the Money Only, You May Not Succeed.** I believe in this one so strongly that I want to replace "may" with "will." You must be in consulting because you believe in what you are doing. Your efforts will have less of a chance of success if you are only trying to promote your business rather than provide a service that you believe in.

10. **Satisfying Your Client Is Your Most Important Responsibility.** This cannot be emphasized too much. It is your job—but beyond that, it leads to more work. A satisfied client is your best marketing weapon. Your goal should be to have your clients marketing for you. A satisfied client leads to repeat work and referrals to other organizations. Satisfying your client is not only your most important responsibility; it is your only responsibility.

11. **Your Personality, Not Your Expertise, Will Land Most Contracts.** Unbelievable, but true. You will be promoting your services and your skills, but time and time again a client will hire someone on "how they come across" rather than their expertise. You might be the best aeronautical systems engineering consultant in the world, but if you come across as arrogant, ignorant, or uninterested, you won't acquire much work. If you have a

personality flaw, correct it. If you do not correct it, no amount of marketing in the world is going to bring business your way.

12. **Dress for Success.** Although this one may sound a bit 1980s outdated, always remember that you are selling you. Your image is critical to selling your consulting services. While "dress for success" conjures up being concerned about whether you wear a navy blue or a gray suit, whether you should add a touch of red to connote power, or making certain your shoes are polished, it goes beyond. Examine your marketing tools—your website, business cards, letterhead, brochures, fliers, and any other paper materials. Are they dressed for success? Designed by professionals? Paper products printed on high-quality paper stock? Have a consistent look? Make sure you are dressed from head to toe and from card to logo.

13. **Quality: First, Last, and Everything in Between.** If I have not stressed how important quality is in everything you do as a consultant, I have not done my job. You should exude quality in all that you do from the first contact to the follow up. With regard to marketing, if you can't do it well, don't bother doing it at all. A brochure with typos, a business card on cheap, flimsy cardstock, a poorly written directory ad, or a poorly delivered conference speech will all detract from the message you are trying to send to your clients and potential clients. Go beyond that. Everyone connected to your office must have a professional demeanor and a client-centered attitude. If they do not, you are losing sales.

The fact that all these Truths are related to marketing and selling, in one way or another, simply underscores the significance that marketing has in your consulting practice.

I hope that this summary delivers a small amount of advice mixed in with a whole lot of excitement. Consulting is an exciting profession. Whether you are preparing for a side hustle or a full-time consulting career in today's gig economy, you are in the driver's seat of your professional journey. No one wants your trip to succeed more than *you* do. *The New Consultant's Quick Start Guide* will send you on the road to your own fulfilling destination.

If you've worked your way through this new Quick Start Guide, you've "wished on paper," and now you have a plan!

Quick Start **LISTS**

Actions I Will Take

Ideas I Have

Questions I Need to Answer

The New Consultant's Quick Start Guide

Electronic Resources

General Consulting Information

- Find an industry magazine at www.consultingmag.com.
- Contact the Institute of Management Consultants at www.IMCUSA.org.
- Find articles, tools, and interviews at Nation1099, www.nation1099.com.
- Contact the Professional Independent Consultants of America (PICA), a national membership organization that provides consultants advice, at www. picanetwork.org.
- Top Consultant is an online talent marketplace for consultants at www.Top-Consultant.com.
- PwC Talent Exchange offers projects within PricewaterhouseCoopers at www. talentexchange.pwc.com.

General Business Information

- The Small Business Administration is a resource for general information such as financial planning: www.sba.gov.
- Looking for entrepreneurial support? Go to www.entrepreneurs.about.com.

- Trying to sort through the business etiquette in other countries? Get information at www.cyborlink.com.

- Need copyright permission? Check www.copyright.com.

- Subscribe to an organizational ethics newsletter at www.ethics.org.

- SCORE offers volunteer support and webinars at www.score.org.

Start-Up Support

Need a quick course that answers all your questions about starting your consulting business? Register for this online course and receive resources before the next class launches. Sign up at www.yourtrainingconsultingbiz.com

- Need help naming your business? Check out the software at www.naming-toolbox.com.

- Considering what insurance to purchase? Try http://www.iii.org/smallbusiness/intro/.

- Access tax considerations related to your business structure at www.IRS.gov.

- Software for writing a business plan can be found at www.business-plan.com.

- Wondering about salary expectations? Check one of these three sites: www.payscale.com, www.careerjournal.com, or www.salaryexpert.com.

- Clarify your marketing message by contacting StoryBrand at www.StoryBrand.com.

- Online survey support is available at www.zoomerang.com.

Reading List

Bellman, G. M. (2002). *The consultant's calling* (2nd ed.). Hoboken, NJ: Wiley.

Biech, E. (2003). *Marketing your consulting services.* Hoboken, NJ: Wiley.

Biech, E. (Ed.). (2007). *The Pfeiffer book of successful team-building tools* (2nd ed.). Hoboken, NJ: Wiley.

Biech, E. (2015). *101 ways to make learning active beyond the classroom.* Hoboken, NJ: Wiley.

Biech, E. (2015). *Training and development for dummies.* Hoboken, NJ: Wiley.

Biech, E. (2016). *Change management training.* Alexandria, VA: ATD Press.

Biech, E. (2017). *The art and science of training.* Alexandria, VA: ATD Press.

Biech, E. (2018a). *ATD's foundations of talent development.* Alexandria, VA: ATD Press.

Biech, E. (2018b). *Starting a talent development program.* Alexandria, VA: ATD Press.

Biech, E. (2019). *The new business of consulting.* Hoboken, NJ: Wiley.

Biech, E., & Swindling, L. B. (2000). *The consultant's legal guide.* Hoboken, NJ: Wiley.

Block, P. (2011). *Flawless consulting* (2nd ed.). Hoboken, NJ: Wiley.

Clark, D. (2017). *Entrepreneurial you.* Boston: Harvard Business Review Press.

Cohen, S. (2017). *The complete guide to building and growing a talent development firm.* Alexandria, VA: ATD Press.

Consulting.Com. (2018). *How much do consultants make?* Retrieved at https://www.consulting.com/consultant-salaries.

Dinnocenzo, D. A. (1999). *101 tips for telecommuters.* San Francisco: Berrett-Koehler.

Daugherty, P., & Wilson, J. (2018). *Human + machine: Reimagining work in the age of AI.* Boston, MA: Harvard Business Review Press.

Dweck, C. (2016). *Mindset: The new psychology of success.* New York: Penguin Random House.

Edwards, R. (2016). *How to write copy that sells: The step-by-step system for more sales, to more customers, more often.* New York: Morgan James Publishing.

Entrepreneur Media Staff. (2015). *Start your own business* (6th ed.). Irvine, CA: Entrepreneur Press.

Evans, H. J., & Biech, E. (2018). *131 Ways to win with accountability: Best practices for driving better results.* Dallas, TX: CornerStone Leadership Institute.

Heisler, K., Southhall, M. & Cardec, L. (2016, December 12). "Randstad US study projects massive shift to agile employment and staffing model in the next decade." Randstad North America, Inc. Retrieved at https://www.randstadusa.com/about/news/randstad-us-study-projects-massive-shift-to-agile-employment-and-staffing-model-in-the-next-decade/.

Henry, P. (2017, February 18). "Why some startups succeed (and why most fail)." *Entrepreneur.* Retrieved at https://www.entrepreneur.com/article/288769.

Hyatt, M. (2018). *Your best year ever: A 5-step plan for achieving your most important goals.* Grand Rapids, MI: Baker Publishing Group.

Lewin, M. D. (1997). *The consultant's survival guide.* Hoboken, NJ: Wiley.

Lewis, L. (2000). *What to charge: Pricing strategies for freelancers and consultants.* Putnam Valley, NY: Aletheia Publications.

Michalowicz, M. (2017). *Profit first: Transform your business from a cash-eating monster to a money-making machine.* New York: Portfolio Penguin.

McGovern, M. (2017) *Thriving in the gig economy.* Wayne, NJ: Career Press.

Miller, D. (2017). *Building a story brand: Clarify your message so customers will listen.* New York: Harper Collins.

Moss, W. (2005). *Starting from scratch: Secrets from 21 ordinary people who made the entrepreneurial leap.* Chicago: Dearborn Trade Publishing.

Phillips, J., & Phillips, P. (Eds.). (2002). *Building a successful consulting practice.* Alexandria, VA: ASTD Press.

Pink, D. (2002). *Free agent nation: The future of working for yourself.* New York: Hachette Book Group.

Pink, D. (2012). *To sell is human: The surprising truth about moving others.* New York: Riverhead Books.

Pofeldt, E. (2018). *The million-dollar one-person business.* New York: Penguin Random House.

Schein, E. (2016). *Humble consulting: How to provide real help faster*. Oakland, CA: Berrett-Koehler Publishers.

Shefsky, L. E. (1994). *Entrepreneurs are made, not born*. New York: McGraw-Hill.

Silberman, M., & Biech, E. (2015). *Active training: A handbook of techniques, designs, case examples, and tips*. Hoboken, NJ: Wiley.

Sobel, A., & Panas, J. (2014). *Power relationships: 26 irrefutable laws for building extraordinary relationships*. Hoboken, NJ: Wiley.

U.S. Small Business Administration. (2016). Small Business Profile. Retrieved at https://www.sba.gov/sites/default/files/advocacy/United_States.pdf

Subscribe to These Periodicals

Consultant News, www.consultant-news.com

Entrepreneur magazine, www.entrepreneur.com/magazine

Fortune magazine, www.fortune.com

Harvard Business Review, www.HBR.org

Wall Street Journal, www.WSJ.com

About the Author

Elaine Biech is a consultant, trainer, and author of the *Washington Post*'s number-one best-seller *The Art and Science of Training*. With more than three decades of experience and 80-plus published books, she has been called "the Stephen King of the training industry."

Elaine is president of ebb associates inc, a strategic implementation and leadership development consulting firm where she helps large organizations work through large-scale change. She has presented at hundreds of national and international conferences and has been featured in publications such as the *Wall Street Journal, Harvard Management Update, Investor's Business Daily,* and *Fortune.* Her books have been published in a dozen languages and several have received national awards.

Among her extensive body of published work are *The New Business of Consulting* and *Training and Development For Dummies.* She has authored the Association for Talent Development (ATD, formerly ASTD)'s flagship publications, *The ASTD Handbook: The Definitive Reference for Training and Development, ATD's Foundations of Talent Development,* and *ATD's Action Guide to Talent Development.*

Elaine is a dedicated lifelong learner who believes that excellence isn't optional. She delights in helping leaders maximize their effectiveness and guiding organizations through the current business churn. Customizing all of her work for individual clients, she conducts strategic planning sessions and implements corporate-wide systems, such as quality improvement, change management, reengineering of business processes, and mentoring programs. She is particularly adept at turning dysfunctional teams into productive ones.

As a consultant, she has provided services globally to the U.S. Navy, China Sinopec, China Telecom, PricewaterhouseCoopers, Banco de Credito Peru, Minera Yanacocha, Lockheed Martin, Newmont Mining, Outback Steakhouse, the Department of Homeland Security, the FAA, Land O' Lakes, McDonald's, Lands' End, Chrysler, Johnson Wax, the Federal Reserve Bank, American Family Insurance, Marathon Oil, Hershey Chocolate, NASA, Newport News Shipbuilding, the Kohler Company, ATD, the American Red Cross, the Association of Independent CPAs, the University of Wisconsin, The College of William and Mary, and hundreds of other public and private sector organizations to prepare them for current challenges.

The recipient of numerous professional awards, Elaine is a consummate training professional who has been instrumental in guiding the talent development profession for most of her career. A long-time volunteer for ATD, she has served on the association's national board of directors, was the recipient of the 1992 ASTD Torch Award, the 2004 ASTD Volunteer Staff Partnership Award, and the 2006 Gordon Bliss Memorial Award. In 2012, she was the inaugural CPLP Fellow Program Honoree from the ASTD Certification Institute. Elaine wrote the first ASTD Training Certification Study Guides.

Elaine was the 1995 Wisconsin Women Entrepreneurs' Mentor Award recipient and has served on the Independent Consultants Association's Advisory Committee. She is currently on the ISA—The Association for Learning Providers board of directors. Elaine is a member of the Center for Creative Leadership's (CCL) board of governors and is the chair of CCL's Research, Evaluation, and Societal Advancement Committee. She is also a member of CCL's executive committee and the editorial board.

Index

NOTE: Page references in *italics* refer to reproducible forms.

Attorneys: and assessing first year of business, 240; hiring, 70–72

Automobile insurance, 86

Azulay, Halelly, 173

B

Balance of life and business: assessment and expectations for, 119–120, 124–125, 243; and enjoyment, 220, 231; flexible rules for, 219–220; and home office location, 131; and identifying imbalance, 219; importance of, 218; interests and hobbies for, 221; managing, 222; personal considerations for consulting plans, 34, 36; privacy issues, 133; reviewing first year of business for, 231–232, 236–238; transition planning for personal life, 119–120, 124–125; vacation time for, 220–221

Banking needs, 82–87, 240

Bellman, Geoff, 219

Bidding. *See* Charging (what to charge)

Biech, Elaine: ebb associates inc, 69, 152, 171, 244–247; *The New Business of Consulting*, 50, 203; Process Tamer, 97

Big Four accounting firms, 104, 105

Billable days, calculating, 52–54

Blogging, 198

Bosses, discussing plans with, 117

Brand. *See* Image

Brokers, insurance, 84

Budgeting: Budget Format, 57, *59*; marketing on shoestring budget, 196–198. *See also* Financial issues

Business cards, 197

Business growth. *See* First-year business survival; Future of business

Businessnamegenerator.com, 67

Business plan, 93–112; appendices to, 108–109; assessment of, 97–98, 111, 117, 240; competitive analysis for, 105–106, 161–162; feedback for, 97–98, 111, 117; for financial projections, 108; market analysis for, 104–105; marketing and sales, 107; necessity of, 93–101; organization and management plan for, 106; printing, 109; reviewing, 111; for services and products, 107–108; structure of, 101–104; using, 109–111. *See also* Marketing plan

C

Calculation method: Calculating What You Require, 50, *51*; defined, 50; determining billable days for, 52–54; types of, 54–57

Cash flow: and assessing first year of business, 239; First-Year Cash-Flow Projection (form), 57, *60*; during start-up phase of consulting, 121–123, *123*; Three-Year Cash-Flow Projection (form), *61*, 62; understanding issues of, 57–62, *59*, *60*, *61*

Casualty insurance, 85

Characteristics of consultants: aptitude for consulting, 9–11; assessing first year of business, 232–234; assessing personal situation for consulting, 119–120; and choosing a consulting career, 3–4; ebb's 13 Truths on, 246–247; and entrepreneurship, 9–11, 13–17, *14–15*, 68, 96–101, 113–117; and motivation for consulting, 21, 26–28

terms for, 47; working for consulting firms, 115. *See also* Characteristics of consultants; Clients; Expenses; Financial issues; First-year business survival; Forms; Future of business; Marketing; Offices; Start-up businesses

Consulting (magazine), 104

Copying and printing: business cards, 197; copyrights, 215; dating of documents, 216; furnishing office for, 131–132; image of printed materials, 196, 197; printing business plan, 109

Copyrights, 215

Corporations, 73–74

Correspondence: Sample Letter, 171; thank you messages/gifts, 156, 217, 218; time management of, 212

Customers. *See* Clients

D

Daily fees, calculating, 54, 56–57, 246

DBA (Doing Business As) certificate, 67

Delight, of clients, 217–218

Department of Labor (state), 88

Design: for business plan, 97, 102; for marketing materials, 163; for websites, 146–147

Disability insurance, 85

"Dressing for success," 247

Dropbox (app), 148

E

ebb associates inc, 69, 152, 171, 244–247

Edwards, Ray, 198, 199

Emergency savings, 62

Employer identification number (EIN), 88

Employment. *See* Permanent employment

Entrepreneurs.about.com, 68

Entrepreneurship: aptitude for, 9–11; and business plan writing, 96–101; Entrepreneur Attitude Survey, 13–17, *14–15*, 100; gaining consulting experience while still employed, 113–117. *See also* Characteristics of consultants

Errors and omission (E&O) insurance, 85

Ethical issues, 224–226

Evernote (app), 148

Executive suites, shared, 128

Expenses: of advertising, 183; apps for, 148; banking and insurance needs, 82–87; financial considerations for consulting plans, 32–33, 36; for marketing, 196–197; Monthly Expense Worksheet/Record, 137, *138*; Personal Expense Plan, 38, *39*; Petty Cash Record, *139*; Start-Up Expenses, *45–46*

Expensify (app), 148

Expertise: applying prior experience to consulting, 4–5; and competency inventory, 6–8; defined, 1; determining market niche, 151–155, 163, 235–236; ebb's 13 Truths on, 245; gaining business expertise, 233–234; gaining consulting experience, 113–117; improving marketing skills, 206; of industry, 158. *See also* Charging (what to charge)

F

Facebook, 197

F-A-I-L (Find Another Ingenious Lead), 233

entities, 75–76; corporations, 73–74; DBA (doing business as) certificate, 67; filing legal documentation for, 88–89; limited liability companies (LLCs), 74; overview, 73; partnerships, 73; sole proprietorships, 73

Liability insurance, 85

Licenses, 87–88

Lifestyle. *See* Balance of life and business; Characteristics of consultants; Family and friends

Limited liability companies (LLCs), 73, 74

LinkedIn, 197

Listening, 244–245

M

Mailchimp (app), 148

Malik, Zayn, 243

Management plan, 106. *See also* Business plan

Marketing, 179–208; ABCs (Assess, Build client base, Contact) of, 180–181; and advertising, 158, 163, 183, 198; by competitors, 163; defined, 179–180; ebb's 13 Truths on, 245–246; for first-year business survival, 216–217; improving skills for, 206; market analysis, 104–105; marketing plan, 107, 181–196; market niche, 151–155, 163, 235–236; and proposals, 200–204; Sample Letter, 171; on shoestring budget, 196–198; tracking clients for, 204, *205*; websites for, 146–149

Marketing plan: ABCs (Assess, Build client base, Contact) for, 180–181;

analyzing present situation for, 182; Annual Marketing Activity, 184, 193, *194*; and assessing first year of business, 241; building steps for, 185–196; business schools for help with, 195; clarifying strategy for, 182; developing, 107; goals for, 182, 183; identifying resources for, 183; implementing, 184; market analysis for, 104–105; monitoring results of, 184; nouns used in, 189–190; written plan for, 181

Meetings: following up after, 176; preparing for appointments with potential clients, 173–174. *See also* Charging (what to charge)

Mistakes, learning from, 233

Monthly Expense Worksheet/Record, 137, *138*

Motivation, ebb's 13 Truths on, 246

N

Namelix.com, 67

Name of business, 66–70, 147

Necessity, as goal for consulting plans, 26–28

Needs analysis, of clients, 155, 176, 200

Networking: building network, 114; Competitor Comparison, 158–160, *159*

The New Business of Consulting (Biech), 50, 203

New clients, finding: preparing for appointments, 173–174; quick ideas for, 172–173; and referrals, 172, 197; research and cold calling, 167–172, *168*. *See also* Clients; Marketing

R

rayedwards.com, 198

Record keeping: and administrative tasks, 212, 242; electronic financial records, 137–140, *138*, *139*, *140*; establishing system for, 136; filing, 135–136; invoicing, 141–143, *143*; for measuring profitability, *144*; organization for, 145; for proposals, 204

Referrals: for new clients, 172; word-of-mouth, 173, 197

Remote firms, for office needs, 128

Remote Year, 128

Rental space for office, 127

Research: ebb's 13 Truths on, 245; for first assignments, 167–172, *168*; interviewing other consultants, 17–18; for writing proposals, 200–201. *See also* Business plan

Retainer basis, 57

Retirement, 47

Revenue: calculating requirement for, 50–57; Calculating What You Require, 50, *51*; Revenue Projections, 139, *140*

Review. *See* Assessment

RFPs (Requests for Proposals), 200

Risk taking, 233

Roe, Dick, 97

S

Sales and selling. *See* Marketing

Savings, 62

Schedule. *See* Time management

ScheduleOnce (app), 148

Second year of business. *See* Future of business

Self-employment: advantages/disadvantages of working alone, 118–119, 158; self-employed consultants, defined, 116. *See also* Consulting; Legal entity of business

Services vs. products, 107–108

Shopify.com, 67

Short-timer attitude, avoiding, 117

Skills. *See* Expertise

Skype (app), 148

Slack (app), 148

Social media, 197–198

Sole proprietorships, 73

Start-up businesses, 65–91; banking and insurance needs of, 82–87; budgeting for, 41–46; costs of, 62; To Do List for, 90; filing legal documentation for, 88–89; hiring accountant and attorney for, 70–72; legal entity of business, 73–82; naming business, 66–70; Start-Up Expenses, *45–46*; zoning laws, licenses, and taxes of, 87–88. *See also* Financial issues; First-year business survival; Future of business

StoryBrand, 146

Students, working with, 195

Subcontractors: as consultants, 2, 115; as employees, 85

Supplies, for office, 133–134

SurveyMonkey (app), 149

Surveys. *See* Interviews, surveys, and questions

T

TalentGrow Show (Azulay), 173

Taxes: Department of Revenue (state), 88; home office deduction, 129

Teachable (app), 149